To _____

From _____

MY FAVORITE RECIPE:

Signed _____

Date _____

FAMOUS
florida! ™
RESTAURANTS & RECIPES

Cover Design and Illustrations by Steele Newman

LaFray Publishing Company
St. Petersburg, Florida

First Edition

For additional copies, use order blanks in
the back of the book or write directly to:

LaFray Publishing Company
P.O. Box 7326
3210-9th Street North
St. Petersburg, Florida 33734
(813) 821-3233

International Standard Book No: 0-942-084-00-4
Library of Congress Catalog Card No.: 81-90604

First Printing: December 1981
Fifth Printing: December 1982

Printed in the United States of America

PUBLISHER: JOYCE LaFRAY
WRITTEN BY: SANDI BROWN
JOYCE LaFRAY
FOOD CONSULTANT: M. JUDY CAMPBELL
ASSISTANT TO THE PUBLISHER: BETTY JO SCHIES

FAMOUS FLORIDA! RESTAURANTS & RECIPES takes you on a driving tour of Florida's finest, most fascinating dining establishments.

We personally met every restaurant owner, sampled what each considered to be his or her outstanding recipes, and toured each restaurant for an inside view of the history and philosophy behind it.

By following these easy-to-prepare recipes, you will be able to recreate in your own home the special occasions, memories and masterful creations you can experience in these great restaurants.

The dining establishments included in FAMOUS FLORIDA! were selected not only for their culinary expertise, but also for their warmth and personal attentiveness. So, when you prepare these recipes, be sure to include a good measure of loving preparation and excellent company to achieve perfect results.

Enjoy YOUR tour of FAMOUS FLORIDA!

Sandi Brown
Joyce LaFray

NOTES FROM THE TEST KITCHEN

We feel Florida's famous restaurants have offered us a fabulous selection of their best recipes including foods indigenous to our lovely tropical state, and others which blend the time-tested secrets of many ethnic cultures. It is our wish that those of you who use this book will do so with complete confidence. You'll enjoy bringing a truly diverse and delicious dining experience to your own table.

Each recipe has been lovingly collected and tested in our kitchens to help insure your success. Tasting was done by a long list of friends that quickly grew as word got around about the delectable recipes. Selections were based on high marks from our testers and tasters and my assurance that they are easy to prepare.

Because of our careful testing procedures, we can promise you excellent results. As with fine food anywhere, great recipes begin with quality ingredients . . . from the first tender green pepper to the freshest fish and carefully selected beef. So we recommend you use the best available in your area.

Some of these recipes suggest serving 3-4 or 6-8 persons to help you in planning for light to hearty appetites. When appropriate we have recommended substitutes readily available in supermarkets or gourmet specialty shops. Other helpful hints will aid you to adapting these prized recipes to your own needs . . . . . an important plus in our fast-paced world.

Bon appetit! We wish you happy cooking, Florida style.

M. Judy Campbell

This book is dedicated to all of our children, Christy, Julie, Claire and Kip, who have shown great patience thoughout this endeavor, and who have always given us ''food for thought.''

INTRODUCTION

FLORIDA — NOT TO BE TAKEN SERIOUSLY!

People from all over the world come to Florida to bask in the sunshine, play in its temperate waters, walk its infinite shoreline of white sand beach, and be entertained by its leisurely pace and carefree atmosphere. To millions of people, Florida is not a state to be taken seriously, after all it's always a holiday!

"CRACKERS"—AND OTHER DELIGHTS

Fortunately, there are those who have discovered Florida's "inner riches" and taken them seriously enough to make our state their home. To an already uniquely varied state, they have contributed their customs, traditions and culinary talents. The result is a fascinating blend of Florida "cracker" (those born and raised in the state) and a potpourri of the flavors and food from all regions of this country, as well as other parts of the world.

YOU ARE WHAT YOU EAT

Our own culinary customs were influenced first by the Seminole Indians, the true discoverers of our bountiful state. Their preparation of our native fruits and vegetables remain a part of our cooking methods today. Spanish explorers were next to influence our food traditions. Their heritage is most present today in the northeast region of the state, particularly St. Augustine, the first established city of the United States.

A constant procession of French, Greek and Minorcan laborers followed. And later, the settlers of nearby tropical islands brought their native food and customs to our potpourri of culinary tradition.

DINING IN FLORIDA, MORE THAN SUSTENANCE

The "Old South" flavor of many of our inherited dishes arrived with the migration of residents from nearby states. And with them, came the "Southern hospitality" that welcomes today's visitors. It is the Southern influence that made dining more than sustenance, but a social occasion of entertainment. We credit our Southern neighbors for our frequent outdoor barbecues and fish fries staged both in backyard seclusion and in the most elite dining establishments in the state.

THE LARGEST VARIETY OF CROPS!

Part of the reason the many culinary traditions of our past have thrived here is the unique geography of this state. Chances are, that which grows in your home state, country or island will grow equally as well, if not more bountifully, in Florida.

Our climate contributes to a year 'round growing season which produces the largest variety of crops in this country — an almost seasonless variety.

Oranges, grapefruit, and kumquats are just the beginning of the fruits of our climate. From the most common apples and strawberries, to the more unusual cocoplums, mangoes, guavas, plantains, and coconuts, Florida produces fruits of the world, for the world. In fact, Florida produces three-fourths of the nation's citrus, and one-fourth of the world's consumption.

MORE THAN JUST VITAMIN C

But man does not live by fruit alone, nor does Florida. Beef, poultry, game, seafood, peanuts, pecans, honey and sugar cane, and, of course, an infinite variety of vegetables are in abundance year 'round. A single county, Dade (home of Miami), produces nearly one-half of the winter vegetables sold in the United States and Canada, November through April. It is no wonder the Spanish discoverers of our state named the region "Florida," meaning "flowered."

DIVERSITY IN CLIMATE AND GEOGRAPHY

If you can tear yourself away from our spectacular beaches, and you really must, you'll discover that aside from mountains, and desert, Florida has no void of climatic or geographic variety. In the north, you'll find lush forests, rolling terrain, even an occasional snowfall during the winter months.

The south is tropical in appearance and climate. The thousands of islands in the Keys could easily be mistaken for Pacific Islands in their secluded habitat and customs. The central and northern regions are covered with rustic woods, lakes and winding rivers. If it weren't for our Spanish Moss lacing the tree limbs, you might imagine yourself to be in the boundary waters of the North.

The coastline areas are as wide in variety as the State's ethnic composition. The warm waters of the Gulf of Mexico and its inhabitants produce a beach line entirely different from the East Coast's Atlantic influence.

AN ABUNDANCE OF DELICACIES

The myriad of waterways allow us an abundance of delicacies from both fresh and salt waters. Bass, grouper, mackerel, pompano, mullet, red snapper, swordfish, shark, sea trout, and bluefish are native to our waters. Shellfish are in abundance as well! Shrimp, Florida lobster, conch, coquinas, stone crab, blue crab, clams and oysters have made Florida their home.

In all, more than 500 species of fish inhabit Florida waters. Fifty of these are commercial varieties, with 200-million pounds being exported each year.

THE NATURAL CHOICE

The most enjoyable way to experience Florida's riches, its foods, customs and people, is through its wide variety of excellent restaurants. A wise professional makes his home where he finds the 'tools' of his trade. And to an enterprising restaurateur, Florida is a natural choice.

Florida has been blessed with the arrival of experienced chefs from all over the world. Combined with the talents of natural masters of the culinary art, those born and raised in our backwoods and seaside communities, your food fair tour of Florida offers an infinite variety of both elegant and 'folksy' cultural dining experiences. Have fun with FAMOUS FLORIDA!

It is not with whom you are bred, but with whom you are fed.

— Spanish

TABLE OF CONTENTS

ART IN STEAKS

BERN'S STEAK HOUSE
tampa

Bern Laxer believes that whatever is done in any field should be done totally, wholeheartedly, and completely. His fanaticism in the field of haute cuisine is why Bern's Steak House in Tampa has become world-famous. What the Sistine Chapel is to art lovers, Bern's is to lovers of fine aged steaks.

Bern decided that if he was to have a restaurant, he would serve the best in steaks, chops, seafood and chicken. He would cultivate his own organic farms to grow fresh and natural vegetables he served his patrons; steaks would be cut to order for each customer; he would custom grind, hand sort and roast his coffees; sprout his own cress for the salads — even grow his own rosemary for the *Chicken Gert*, a popular entrée named in honor of his wife. If you asked, Bern could tell you the life history of each of your entrées.

Bern's Steak House is not to be outdone in the quality of its wine cellar, either. The cellar contains at least a half million bottles, resulting in a winelist that is almost the size of Webster's Unabridged! Bern and his wife, Gert, knew nothing about wines when they started in the restaurant business almost thirty years ago, but they approached the task with zeal and have now created an oenologist's nirvana.

Heavenly steaks, the freshest vegetables imaginable, and

ultra-rich desserts are served to you by Bern-trained waiters amid gilt Rococo opulence. The decor is almost overwhelming. Bern admits he chose Rococo to attract attention, although this impressive decor is only of momentary interest. The real masterpieces are not on canvas - they are the pleasing palette of palate pleasing vegetables surrounding a filet mignon that would give the Mona Lisa something to *really* smile about! In the Tampa Bay area, which boasts hundreds of excellent dining choices, Bern's Steak House remains one of the first replies to the thousands of visitors who ask, "What is the best restaurant in the area?"

Take the Howard-Armenia exit off I-275 in downtown Tampa and go south on Armenia to Swann Avenue, then left onto Swann to Howard. Turn right on Howard. Bern's is located at 1208 South Howard.

Reservations Necessary.

STEAK TARTARE
(To Be Served Immediately)

5½	oz steak (as fresh, lean and red as possible)
4	T. shallots (finely chopped)
2	T. green pepper (peeled and finely chopped)
2	T. red wine mixture (80% red wine/20% cream sherry)
1	t. fine herbs (Spice Island)
¼	t. salt
1/8	t. freshly ground pepper
1	egg yolk
4	celery strips (for garnish)
4	onion slices (for garnish)
	parsley (for garnish)

1. Hand-chop steak into small pieces, removing any strains of fat or gristle.
2. Chop shallots and green peppers into steak so that steak is chopped a second time - or put in food processor 7 seconds.
3. Add other ingredients except for garnish and blend well (do not purée).
4. Garnish with celery strips, onion slices and parsley. Serve with brown bread wedges toasted with caraway butter.

Serves: 4 - 2 oz servings or 8 - 1 oz servings
Preparation: 10 minutes

"Perfection in a tartare! !"

– NOTES –

CAESAR SALAD
(Prepare Caesar Oil and Croutons in Advance)

1	clove fresh garlic (peeled)
6	large anchovies (finely chopped)
2/3	cup Bern's Caesar Oil (Recipe to follow)
4	T. lemon juice (2 lemons)
	freshly ground black pepper
2-3	coddled eggs (boiled 1 minute)
1	cup freshly grated Parmesan cheese (or blend of Parmesan and Romano)
1	large head Romaine lettuce torn in salad size pieces (enough for 4 servings)
1	cup Bern's Garlic Croutons (Recipe to follow)

— SALAD —

1. Rub large wooden bowl with garlic clove.
2. In the wooden bowl, mix together anchovies, Caesar Oil, lemon juice, pepper and egg until well blended.
3. Add Romaine pieces. Toss to coat every piece. Add ¾ of the cheese, reserving remaining cheese to sprinkle on salad. Toss again.
4. To serve, place in individual chilled bowls and sprinkle with croutons and cheese.

— CAESAR OIL —

1	cup fine quality olive oil
½	oz. garlic (peeled, 1-2 cloves)
	oil from 2 oz. tin of anchovies
½	anchovy

1. Purée. Remember to use only 2/3 of this for salad recipe. (Yield: 1 cup).

— CROUTONS —

4	slices tight knit bread (allow to dry out)
2-4	garlic cloves (peeled)
	Spike seasoning (available in health food stores)

-continued-

1. Put a small "dab" of Spike seasoning in a dish, then dip the peeled garlic in the seasoning and rub the bread (both sides) with the seasoned garlic.

2. Cut in small cubes and toast slightly. (Yield: 1 cup)

Serves: 4
Preparation: 15 minutes

"The special Caesar Oil and croutons make this one of the best ever!"

— NOTES —

BRAZILIAN SNOW

4 oz. freshest coffee beans (roasted but unground)
1 pint vanilla ice cream (best quality)
whipped cream

1. To prepare this simple dessert, you will need a small grain grinder, like a Moulinex. Grind the coffee as finely as possible.*
2. Sprinkle a medium coating of the coffee, mixing ice cream carefully with the coffee. Scoop the coffee and ice cream as many as 7-8 times.
3. Top with a dollop of whipped cream. Garnish with a sprinkle of the ground coffee and a cherry.

Serves: 3-4
Preparation: 2-3 minutes. Make as quickly as possible!

*"For maximum coffee flavor, Bern suggests using coffee no longer than 5-10 minutes after grinding. If you do not have a Moulinex, we suggest having your coffee shop grind it in a Turkish grind. DASH HOME WITH IT!"

— NOTES —

Bon Appétit

"Bon Appétit" is the hearty greeting from your waiter as he proudly places taste-tempting continental cuisine on your table. Bon Appétit is also the name of Dunedin, Florida's newest and most exclusive enclave of fine dining. With its million-dollar view of St. Joseph's Sound, Bon Appétit is quickly becoming a favorite spot for area gourmets.

One can enjoy the spectacular waterfront sunsets while savoring delicate seafood crepes and other culinary master-pieces. It is a place to relax and enjoy the refreshing little differences created by conscientious attention to detail. Pale pink table linens, fresh flowers in cut glass vases, elegant stem-ware and attentive, helpful waiters are just some of the lovely surprises at Bon Appétit A "Members Only" Winecellar is a unique feature — where for a nominal fee guests can maintain their own private stock. If you haven't your own bottle, we recommend *Corton Charlemagne 1971*, a luscious white wine, or a sparkling *Henkell Trocken Vintage.*

International chef Karl Heinz Riedl, a member of the prestigious *Chaine des Rotisseurs* has a long history of tanta-lizing the taste buds of celebrities such as Queen Elizabeth, Pablo Picasso, Charles DeGaulle and Elizabeth Taylor.

Bon Appétit is a dining establishment that features Euro-pean haute cuisine and attention to detail combined with American practicality and efficiency — a successful marriage of the Old World and the New!

Take State Road 580 into Dunedin, just north of Clearwater. Go as far west as possible on S.R. 580. When you're in sight of the waterfront, the Jamaica Inn is on your right. Bon Appétit is located on the water-front at the westernmost part of the Inn.

Reservations Suggested.

CRÊPES BON APPÉTIT
(Specialté de la Maison)

1   recipe crepes *
1   recipe hollandaise *

— FILLING —
1   onion (diced)
1   cup celery (diced)
2   T. butter
½   cup flour
1   bay leaf
1   cup small shrimp (cooked)
1   cup small scallops (cooked reserving stock to yield 2 cups)
½   cup white wine
½   cup cream
     salt and pepper to taste

1. In a skillet sauté onions and celery in butter.
2. Add flour, mix well. Cook 2 minutes. Pour in enough stock to make 2 cups medium thick sauce.
3. Add bay leaf, simmer 20 minutes, stirring.
4. Add seafood, wine and cream. Season with salt and pepper.
5. Place 1-2 T. filling on each crêpe. Fold in sides and roll up. Place seam side down in au gratin dishes.
6. Top with hollandaise sauce and place under broiler until golden brown.

*See Glossary
Serves: 8
Preparation: 30 minutes
Cooking: 20/5

"A rich and delightful seafood dish!"

ENGLISH SOLE PROVENÇALE

4	small sole (washed, cleaned and trimmed)
1	t. salt
¼	t. pepper
	juice of 1 lemon
¼	cup flour
2	T. olive oil

– SAUCE –

1	shallot (chopped)
1	clove garlic (chopped)
3	T. butter
2	large tomatoes (peeled, chopped and drained)

1. Season fish with salt and pepper. Sprinkle with lemon juice and dip lightly in flour.
2. Heat oil in skillet. Cook fish until golden brown on both sides (about 10 minutes). Remove to hot platter, keeping hot.

– SAUCE –

3. Sauté shallot and garlic in butter for 2 minutes. Add chopped tomatoes. Cook 5 minutes more. Pour over fish to serve.

Serves: 4
Preparation: 10 minutes
Cooking: 17-20 minutes

"A simple recipe for good fresh fish."

– NOTES –

LAMB CHOPS CHAMPILLON

8	loin or rib lamb chops
2	T. butter
1	large onion (sliced)
1½	lb. potatoes (washed, peeled and sliced thin)
1	bay leaf
½	t. thyme leaves
	salt and pepper to taste
1½	cups bouillon
2	T. parsley (chopped)
4	T. bread crumbs

1. Sauté chops in butter. Cover pan. Cook until meat is delicately browned on both sides.
2. Add onions to meat. Cook 5 minutes.
3. Add potatoes, bay leaf, thyme, salt, pepper and bouillon. Cover and let cook until meat is tender.
4. Remove chops to a casserole dish. Garnish with the potatoes and onion. Sprinkle with the parsley and bread crumbs. Brown under broiler until top is golden.

Serves: 4
Preparation: 15 minutes
Cooking: 30/5 minutes

"Wonderful country flavor!"

—NOTES —

MEDALLIONS OF BABY VEAL JEAN LAFITTE

1½ lbs. veal medallions (pounded thin)
    scant amount of flour for dusting
2   T. shallots (minced)
6   T. butter
1   cup heavy cream (not ultra pasteurized)
4   T. bourbon
    salt and pepper to taste
8   shrimp (peeled, deveined with tail left on, butterflied
    and cooked)
    spinach noodles

1. Sauté shallots in butter for 2 minutes. Add flour-dusted medallions. Sauté each side for 2-3 minutes. Remove to warm platter.
2. Stir in cream and simmer (do not boil) until slightly thickened. Add bourbon and simmer for 2 minutes more. Taste for seasoning.
3. To serve place shrimp on veal. Pour sauce evenly over all.

Serves: 4
Preparation: 15 minutes
Cooking: 12 minutes

"Bon Appetit serves this with spinach pasta for color. It's a simple but beautiful preparation."

– NOTES –

sarasota/palm beach

A perennial award winner and favorite among Sarasota residents and visitors is striking Café L'Europe on St. Armands Key. The best elements of a European café are tenderly combined to enhance dining pleasure. The warmth of brick and shades of pink and rose table linens are strikingly accented by an abundance of foliage. Fresh cut flowers add a festive continental touch, and in such masses that could pass this dining haven as a florist shop. The owners are known to have ordered as many as 4000 tulips from Holland for display in every possible nook.

The café theme is echoed with bentwood chairs and a colorful delft tile buffet. A cheery and charming effect.

The cuisine of Café L'Europe is continental. There's a slight favoring of the German with such entrées as *Wienerschnitzel*, one of six veal offerings. *Brandied Duckling*, *Red Snapper "Belle Meuniere"* and *Tournedos Mignon* round out the entrées. *Escargots Bourguignonne* and *Seafood Coquille Gratinee* are just two of the luscious hot appetizers. Eight cold appetizers including *Imported White Asparagus* and *Fresh Smoked Trout* are available.

Lest we forget the desserts — a homestyle *Key Lime Pie* is a favorite plus traditional pastries and cheese cake. A variety of other select delights are available to enjoy while sipping the exotic special coffees. The *Alexandria*, with its *Creme de*

Cacao, the *Italiano with Strega* or the potent *Cafe' L'Europe* with its blend of Creme de Menthe and Cacao are the perfect dinner denouément.

No wonder this delightful restaurant is the recipient of major award after award including the Holiday Magazine Award for dining excellence and Florida Trend Magazine's Golden Spoon Award!

Cafe' L'Europe and its little touch of Europe is the work of Europeans Titus Letschert and Norbert Goldner who have kept busy with Cafe' L'Europe in Sarasota as well as the youthful Cafe' L'Europe in Palm Beach. We met with Titus, a suave and cosmopolitan man whom one might expect to be more at home on the cover of a fashion magazine than involved in restaurant operations.

On the mall upstairs from Saks on famed Worth Avenue is the Palm Beach Cafe' L'Europe — equally as lovely but a touch more sophisticated and upbeat. There's an art nouveau flavor to the decor.

It's a pleasure to dine in its fashionable pampered formality. Of course this might be expected since the Esplanade shopping mall, of which it is a part, includes among other shops, Cartier Jewelers, Charles Jourdan of Paris and Ralph Lauren. It naturally follows that the beautiful people of Palm Beach should deserve a meal as fashionable as the clothes!

A morning of shopping in St. Armands Key or Palm Beach's exclusive shops, a leisurely lunch, lingering over *Coffee Alexandria*. . .those special moments. . . Cafe' L'Europe.

To find Café L'Europe in St. Armands Key, follow U.S. 41 south from Tampa/St. Petersburg or north from Naples/Fort Myers to S.R. 780, Sarasota. Then head west to the beaches and St. Armands. Café L'Europe is located in the first section of shops to the right. In Palm Beach, the restaurant is located at 150 Worth Avenue at Esplanade. Reservations are Suggested at both locations.

SWEETBREADS "PRINCESE"

6   12 oz. sweetbreads (preferably calf)
1   gallon clear veal stock
1   stalk celery, cut in lg. chunks
1   carrot, cut in lg. chunks
1   onion
4   whole peppercorns
1   t. salt
½   cup vinegar
     flour
     butter
     salt, pepper to taste
     egg wash (2 eggs beaten and strained)

— HOLLANDAISE SAUCE —
6   large egg yolks
8   t. lemon juice
6   t. water
2   cups butter (melted)
     dash of salt
     dash of white pepper
     dash of cayenne

—GARNISH —
24   whole white asparagus
6   thin ham slices

1.   Soak sweetbreads in cold water for 30 minutes. Drain.
2.   In a large pot, combine the veal stock, vegetables, pep-
     percorns, and salt. Cook over low to medium heat.
3.   As the stock begins to get hot, add the sweetbreads and
     vinegar. Poach for 20-25 minutes. Remove from heat
     and cool.
4.   After sweetbreads have cooled, remove from stock, trim
     excess fat and skin, then slice or butterfly.
5.   Season with salt and pepper. Lightly flour each side, and
     dip in egg wash.

-continued-

6.   Sauté in hot skillet until each side is golden brown.
7.   Remove from skillet and set each portion atop a slice of
     ham.

— HOLLANDAISE SAUCE —

8.   Combine egg yolks, lemon juice, water and seasonings in
     a double boiler on medium heat. Whip with a wire whisk
     until very fluffy.
9.   Remove from heat and whip butter into mixture, a little
     at a time. Do not keep very hot, or mixture will break
     or curdle.

— GARNISH —

10. Garnish each sweetbread with 4 white asparagus and top
     with hollandaise. Serve.

Serves: 6
Preparation: 30/30 minutes
Cooking: 1½ hours

"Classic approach to preparing sweetbreads!"

— NOTES —

ROAST DUCKLING WITH BRANDIED CHERRY SAUCE

3   ducks (4-5 lbs. each)
3   oranges
    salt, white pepper (to taste)

— BRANDIED CHERRY SAUCE —
2   17 oz. cans bing cherries
1   cup currant jelly
2   cups orange juice (fresh squeezed)
½   cup red wine
3-4 T. cornstarch (mixed slightly with water)
½   cup brandy

1. Preheat oven to 375°.
2. Trim away excess fat and wings from duckling.
3. Set duck in a roasting pan on an open rack. Squeeze the juice from half an orange on both sides of duck, and place squeezed orange inside duck cavity.
4. Sprinkle salt and pepper over duckling and inside cavity.
5. Roast for 2 hours, rotating every half hour.
6. After roasting, cool slightly, split duck and remove rib bones.

— SAUCE —
7. Strain juice from cherries and save both. In a saucepan combine the cherry juice, jelly, orange juice, and wine, and cook over medium heat.
8. As sauce begins to boil, skim the top, and add the starch mixture. Cook until sauce thickens, and then boil a few minutes to cook out the starch.
9. Stir in cherries and brandy.
10. Warm duckling. Serve sauce over duck with a twist of orange slice for garnish.

Serves: 6
Preparation: 1 hour
Cooking/Baking: 1-2 hours

"Beautiful to serve and absolutely mouth-watering to eat!"

VEAL CHOP ORLOFF

6   veal chops (10-12 oz. each)
6   T. butter
    flour
    salt and pepper to taste

— WHITE SAUCE —
2   cups veal stock
1   cup heavy cream
6   T. roux*
    salt and white pepper to taste

— SAUCE —
2   T. butter
½   lb. mushrooms (chopped)
10   medium shallots (chopped)
3   cups white sauce
1   T. sherry
    salt, white pepper to taste

1.   Preheat oven to 400°.
2.   Lightly flour each chop. Season with salt and pepper.
3.   Sauté chops in a hot skillet, until golden brown on each side.
4.   Finish cooking veal chops in oven for 10 minutes.

— WHITE SAUCE —
5.   Cook roux (equal amounts of fat and flour) over low heat. Add veal stock, cream, and seasoning. Simmer for 10 minutes.

— SAUCE —
6.   Sauté mushrooms and shallots in a hot pan until cooked.
7.   Add white sauce and continue cooking for a few minutes. Add sherry and season to taste.
8.   Top each chop with sauce. Serve.

*See Glossary
Serves: 6
Preparation: 15 minutes
Cooking: 20/15 minutes

"Easy to prepare and the creamy mushroom sauce transports one to Cafe L'Europe."

APPLE PANCAKE CAFE L'EUROPE

— BATTER —
1   cup flour
½   t. salt
1/3 cup milk
6   eggs
½   t. vanilla
2   Red Delicious apples (peeled, cored, and sliced)
½   lb. butter (clarified)*
3   T. cinnamon sugar (2T. sugar mixed with 1T. cinnamon)
     ligonberries or preserves

1. Place flour and salt in bowl of electric mixer. Beat in milk, then two of the eggs until smooth. Turn off mixer and add remaining eggs and vanilla. Let sit for 20 minutes.
2. Preheat oven to 425º. Clarify the butter.
3. Turn on mixer and blend batter for 10 seconds.
4. Add ½ clarified butter to a 10" skillet and sauté one-half of the apples for 1 minute. Add one-half of the batter, tilting pan to smooth excess. Flip over after one side is brown.
5. Sprinkle with 1T. cinnamon sugar and place in oven 10 minutes or until puffed and golden brown.
6. Repeat for second pancake. Serve immediately with Lingonberries or preserves.

Serves: 2-4
Preparation: 25 minutes
Cooking: 15 minutes

"You will agree these puffed pancakes make a luscious dessert!"

SOUTH SEAS PLANTATION *captiva island*

Entertaining native instincts, yet enjoying some modern comforts, Chadwick's restaurant at the South Seas Plantation caters to your inclinations. Located at the very tip of Captiva Island off the coast of Ft. Myers, South Seas Plantation is an outpost reminiscent of a Michener paradise. It's all very civilized, but at times the feeling is just this side of "Dr. Livingston, I presume", in the lush tropical underbrush.

The award-winning Chadwick's was named for Clarence Chadwick who bought Captiva and the north end of Sanibel Island in the early 1900's as a Key Lime Plantation. Now it's a famous Florida hideaway famed for its rustic charm. Chadwick's is a popular spot for guests of the resort as well as locals who can't resist Friday seafood buffets and Sunday brunches of palatial proportions.

The decor is "back-porch" chic from the turn of the century with lots of high back golden oak chairs and abundant greenery. There's a "garden-gazebo" room with white lattice accents, an old-time saloon, plus a modern lounge where the island's night life swings into action.

For those who tire of the golfing, boating, swimming, and shelling featured at the popular resort, there's always diving — into a platter of *Beer Batter Shrimp* or *Veal Del Sol*. And if you have promised yourself a rewarding dinner of fresh and tender seafood, your tastebuds won't be disappointed. Chadwick's features several seafood dishes on the menu, as fresh as if it were your own catch and prepared in ways even your wishful imagination never dreamed of.

Chadwick's makes all your dining dreams come true.

To reach South Seas Plantation and Chadwick's, take Route 41 in Fort Myers west till it meets State Road 865. At the intersection of S.R. 865 and S.R. 867, take 867 west over the toll bridge onto Sanibel Island. Go northwest on Periwinkle Road, then north onto Palm Ridge Road. Palm Ridge Road runs into Sanibel-Captiva Road. Go north on Sanibel-Captiva Road until you reach South Seas Plantation, which is going to seem like it takes forever. South Seas Plantation is at the northernmost part of Captiva Island. The island is over 15 miles long.

Reservations Suggested.

SALMON AMBROSIA

6	salmon fillets
1/3	cup flour for salmon
¼	cup butter
1	lb. shrimp (cooked and deveined)

— SPINACH MIXTURE —

½	cup onion (diced)
1	stick butter (4 oz.)
1	lb. spinach (frozen, chopped and cooked)
1	cup heavy cream
	salt and white pepper to taste
	nutmeg to taste
1	oz. Pernod
1	T. Worcestershire sauce
3	oz. flour

— HOLLANDAISE SAUCE —
(With Mustard and Dill)

6	egg yolks
1	t. lemon juice
	Tabasco to taste
1/8	t. salt
1	lb. butter (clarified)*
1/8	cup fresh dill (chopped)
3	oz. Dijon mustard

— SPINACH MIXTURE —

1. Sauté onion in half of butter. Add drained spinach, cream and all seasonings. Bring to boil. Blend remaining butter with 3 oz. flour. Whip into boiling spinach mixture. Simmer for 10 minutes. Correct seasonings (should be thick). Set aside.

— HOLLANDAISE —

2. In a double boiler, place egg yolks, lemon juice, Tabasco,

*See Glossary   -continued-

salt, and whisk until volume increases and is thick and fluffy.

3.   Remove from heat. Whisk in butter slowly until blended. Add dill and mustard. Mix well. Keep warm.
Yield: 2¼ cups.

— SALMON —

4.   Lightly flour salmon. Salt and pepper to taste. Top with butter and shrimp, evenly divided among fillets. Bake 5-7 minutes at 350⁰.

5.   Arrange on bed of spinach mixture. Spoon hollandaise sauce over salmon.

Serves: 6
Preparation: 15 minutes
Cooking: 10 minutes salmon
          5-7 minutes sauce

"Ambrosia means 'exquisitely gratifying in taste'. This preparation is aptly named!"

— NOTES —

VEAL DEL SOL

— VEAL —

1¾ lbs. veal scalloppine (flattened well, to make 6 portions)
    flour
    salt and pepper to taste
6-12 artichoke heart quarters
6   thin slices prosciutto or ham
6   thin slices mozzarella cheese
6   T. Parmesan (grated)
¼   lb. butter

— MARSALA SAUCE —

1   cup Marsala
1   T. shallots (chopped)
1   bay leaf
    pinch of thyme
1   lb. mushrooms (sliced)
1   cup beef stock
1   T. cornstarch (dissolved in 1 T. water)

— MARSALA SAUCE —

1. In a sauce pan bring wine, shallots, bay leaf and thyme to boil. Reduce* by one half.
2. Add mushrooms, and beef stock. Simmer 5 minutes.
3. Bring back to boil and add cornstarch mixture slowly. Slowly stirring well. Remove from heat and keep warm.

*See Glossary
Yield: about 2 cups
Preparation: 10 minutes
Cooking: 15 minutes

— VEAL DEL SOL —

4. Flour, salt and pepper veal. Shake off excess. Sauté on both sides and place on oven proof platter.
5. Place a spoonful of sauce on each piece of veal. Then add 1-2 artichokes on each piece and top with 1 slice ham, mozzarella and 1T. Parmesan.
6. Bake in hot oven at 400º for 5 minutes or until cheese is melted.
7. Top with more sauce and serve remaining on the side.

Serves: 6
Preparation: 15 minutes
Cooking: 15/5 minutes

"Marsala and veal are naturals together. The remaining ingredients are reminiscent of Cordon Bleu. Delightful!"

— NOTES —

CHICKEN CAPTIVA
(First Make Garlic Butter & Dijon Sauce)

6	chicken breasts (skinned and boned)
	salt and pepper to taste
¼	cup flour
½	lb. butter
18	shrimp (cooked and sliced in half)
6	oz. mozzarella cheese
6	green onions (sliced thin)
6	strips bacon (cooked and crumbled)
4	oz. garlic butter
12	oz. Dijon sauce

— GARLIC BUTTER —

¼	lb. butter
1	clove garlic
1	t. chablis
1	t. Worcestershire
6	sprigs parsley
1	t. lemon juice
1	T. bread crumbs
1	t. shallots
½	T. Pernod
	salt and pepper to taste

— DIJON SAUCE —

¼	cup chablis
1	bay leaf
	pinch of thyme
½	t. Worcestershire
½	T. shallots (minced)
½	t. lemon juice
4	oz. Dijon mustard
1	pint heavy cream
1	T. flour
1	T. butter
1/8	cup sherry
	dash of Tabasco
	salt to taste

-continued-

— GARLIC BUTTER —

1. Purée garlic butter ingredients in blender or food processor. Chill. Yield: 6 oz.

"Great on steaks and fish also!"

— DIJON SAUCE —

2. In a sauce pan: bring to a boil the chablis, bay leaf, thyme, Worcestershire, shallots, and lemon juice. Reduce* by one half.
3. Add mustard and cream. Bring to a boil.
4. Make a roux* of butter and flour. Drop into boiling sauce and whisk to blend. Reduce until thick.
5. Add sherry. Simmer for 2 minutes. Season with salt and Tabasco. Keep warm.

— CHICKEN —

(Now let's put it together)

6. Sprinkle chicken with salt and pepper. Dredge in flour and brown on both sides until just done. Place on oven proof platter.
7. Top each breast with sliced shrimp. Top with 1T. garlic butter and 1 oz. cheese. Bake until cheese is lightly browned.
8. Place hot Dijon sauce on warmed serving platter. Arrange breasts on sauce. Sprinkle tops with sliced green onions and crumbled bacon.

*See Glossary
Serves: 6
Preparation: 40 minutes
Cooking: 15 minutes

"An elegant way to serve chicken. Well worth the effort. All it needs is a cool green salad and crusty french bread!"

The Colony Restaurant

Has your beach picnic ever included Prime *Rack of Lamb Mephisto* or Homemade *Key Lime Pie?* The Colony Restaurant on Longboat Key offers memorable gulfside dining with extravagant culinary delights. Endless sets of tennis and romping in the surf build up hearty appetites, easily satisfied by *Swordfish Beurre Naté, Veal Marsala* or tender *Baby Scallops* prepared "as you wish" by Chef Frank Caldwell. Manager Michael Klauber has made quite a few changes in the restaurant to keep pace with the sophisticated patrons. A Champagne Festival, a sumptuous Sunday Brunch and one of the most extensive wine lists in Florida are just a few of his smashing successes at the beautiful and exclusive Colony Beach and Tennis Resort.

Peach tablecloths and napkins decorate tables surrounded by a myriad of hanging plants and fresh flowers flattering the dining room. As diners leisurely contemplate dazzling Florida sunsets, attentive professional waiters scurry about laden with heavenly appetizers and desserts. There's no "nose in the air" formality surrounding the Colony Restaurant - just an air of relaxation and happiness.

Leave your snorkeling equipment and beach ball on the patio. The Colony Beach and Tennis Resort gives "going to the beach" a new meaning! And, the Colony Restaurant makes a day at the beach an elegant affair. After all, man should not live by hamburgers and hot dogs alone!

The Colony Restaurant is located at the Colony Beach and Tennis Resort on Longboat Key off the coast of Sarasota. At the intersection of U.S. Highway 41 and S.R. 780, take S.R. 780 west over the drawbridge to St. Armand's Circle. Go one quarter turn around the circle to Boulevard of Presidents (780). Head north for less than one mile and cross the bridge to Longboat Key. The Colony Beach and Tennis Resort is on the left side about 2 miles after the bridge.

Reservations Suggested.

DILL DRESSING

2	eggs
4	T. pure olive oil
1	t. garlic (minced)
2	t. Spanish onion (minced)
1	t. poupon mustard
2	T. fresh dill weed (chopped)
2	oz. heavy cream
3	T. red wine vinegar
1	t. sugar
1	t. salt
½	t. white pepper

1. Mix all ingredients well and beat for 15 minutes until creamy. Yield: 1 cup.
2. Toss with your favorite selection of salad greens.

Serves: 4
Preparation: 25 minutes

"Tangy and good!"

— NOTES —

POACHED SWORDFISH BEURRE NATÉ

6	8 oz. swordfish steaks

– COURT BOUILLON –

2	qts. water
½	clove garlic
½	white onion
2	bay leaves
1	carrot
2	stalks celery
½	lemon
2	t. salt
2	t. pepper
6	sprigs parsley
	fish scraps (from steaks)

– BEURRE NATÉ –

½	cup water
1	cup chablis
½	cup shallots (chopped)
4	t. red wine vinegar
	juice of 2 lemons
2	bay leaves
2	T. salt
1	T. white pepper
1½	cups sweet butter
1	cup heavy cream

– COURT BOUILLON –

1. Combine bouillon ingredients in large pot, cook 1 hour on medium heat. Cool and strain.
2. Return to boil, reduce to simmer.

-continued-

— BEURRE NATÉ —

3. Combine all ingredients except butter and cream. Cook on low heat until contents are reduced to 1½ cups (about 35-40 minutes).
4. Fold in butter and cream.

— SWORDFISH —

5. Poach steaks in court bouillon nine (9) minutes. Remove immediately.
6. Pour sauce over steaks, garnish appropriately and serve immediately.

Serves: 6 as entrée - 12 as first course
Preparation: 10 minutes
Cooking: 1½ hours

"Superb! If you have not tried swordfish, start with this. It will be in your cooking repertoire forever!"

— NOTES —

VEAL SCALLOPPINE a la MILANESE
(Prepare Sauce in Advance)

— VEAL —

2	lbs. veal medallions (pounded thin)
	flour
½	stick butter

— MILANESE SAUCE —

2	large tomatoes (peeled and chopped)
4	oz. tongue (julienne cut*)
2⁻	oz. smoked ham (julienne)
1	cup fresh mushrooms (julienne)
1	large Spanish onion (julienne)
1	T. butter
1	T. fresh ground black pepper
1	T. salt (add gradually according to your taste)
2	T. garlic (minced)
2	T. oregano
2	cups beef stock

— MILANESE SAUCE —

1. Sauté tomatoes, tongue, ham, mushrooms and onion in butter.
2. Stir in seasonings and add stock. Simmer 45 minutes.
   Yield: 3 cups

— VEAL —

3. Dust veal lightly with flour, and sauté in as much butter as needed. 3-4 minutes each side.
4. To serve, place cooked veal on warmed platter and top with sauce. Serve extra sauce on side.

*See Glossary
Serves: 6
Preparation: 10 minutes
Cooking: 45 minutes 8 minutes

"This sauce is great. Try it on the pasta of your choice!"

On the Gulf of Mexico

Entrance to the Columbia Restaurant

Columbia

SPANISH RESTAURANTS

GEM of

tampa

With its glazed Spanish tiles, shimmering like jewels in the sultry Florida sun, the Columbia Restaurant truly is "the Gem of Spanish Restaurants". Moorish-style lattice porticoes and ornate fountains grace the entrance of this massive restaurant which covers an entire city block in Tampa's historic Ybor City district. Original founder of the Columbia, Casimirio Hernandez, Sr., passed on the ownership to his son, who later invited his son-in-law and present owner, Cesar Gonzmart into the family business.

Since 1905, Tampa's Latin community has gathered at the Columbia for good food and fellowship. Its eleven dining rooms are vibrant with explosive laughter and animated discussions in both Spanish and English. Adults and children enjoy dining on Spanish and Cuban delicacies amid opulent surroundings.

If you give the Columbia a few day's notice, they will even serve the traditional Cuban-style whole roast suckling pig! Lively floor shows and Cesar's flamboyant violin virtuosity highlight the evening. Music enthusiasts crowd the café, with its turn of the century furnishings, to hear live popular and jazz groups.

It is no surprise that the Columbia has won so many awards including the 1981 Mobil Travel Guide Four Star Award and Florida Trend Magazine's Golden Spoon Award. It's a place brimming with life truly reflecting the personality and the traditions of the Gonzmart family. Robust food and a zest for life are the qualities that have kept the Columbia Restaurant in the hearts of Tampa residents for over 75 years!

The Columbia is located at the corner of 7th Avenue and 21st Street in Tampa's Ybor City district. Take I-275 north to I-4 and exit at the 21st Street exit (Exit 1), then travel south to 7th Avenue.

Reservations Suggested.

SPANISH BEAN SOUP
(Soak Beans Overnight With 1T. Salt)

¼	lb. garbanzos (about a cup)
1	T. salt
8	oz. ham (cut in chunks)
2	qts. water
4	oz. salt pork* (sliced)
1	onion (chopped)
3	medium potatoes (quartered)
2	Chorizos (Spanish sausage-sliced)

1. Wash beans thoroughly and soak them overnight with 1T. salt and enough water to cover.
2. Next morning, drain salted water from beans, add 2 qts. water and the ham to beans. Simmer 45 minutes.
3. Meanwhile, sauté salt pork and add onions, stirring.
4. Add onion and pork mixture, and potatoes to the beans. Cook until potatoes are done.
5. Remove from heat. Add Chorizos.

*Bacon may be substituted but drain off grease.

Serves: 4
Preparation: 10 minutes
Cooking: 1-1½ hours

"A hearty meal! !"

− NOTES −

RED SNAPPER "ALICANTE"

2   lbs. red snapper
2   spanish onions (sliced)
4   cloves garlic (minced)
½   cup olive oil
1   cup sauterne wine
¾   cup brown sauce*
1   pinch of pepper
1   t. salt
4   green peppers (sliced)

— FOR GARNISH —
8   slices eggplant (breaded and fried)
8   Shrimp Supreme (Recipe to follow)
¼   cup sliced toasted almonds
     parsley

1. Make Shrimp Supreme recipe.
2. Place snapper on top of onions and garlic in a casserole.
3. Over the fish, pour the olive oil, wine, and brown sauce. Sprinkle with salt and a pinch of pepper and top with green pepper slices.
4. Bake in 350º oven, 25 minutes or until done.

— GARNISH —
5. Garnish with eggplant, Shrimp Supreme, almonds and parsley.

*See Glossary
Serves: 4
Preparation: 10 minutes
Cooking: 25-35 minutes
"Beautiful to serve! Great tasting!"
— NOTES —

-continued-

COLUMBIA SHRIMP SUPREME

16	large raw shrimp (peeled and deveined)
	juice of 1 lemon
1	t. garlic powder
1	t. salt
½	t. pepper
8	strips bacon
1	egg
½	cup milk
	flour

1. Pat shrimp dry and marinate in lemon juice, garlic, salt and pepper for 10 minutes.
2. Cut bacon strips in half, wrap around shrimp and secure with a tooth pick.
3. Beat together egg and milk and dip shrimp in batter. Roll in flour.
4. Deep fry at 300° until golden brown (about 5-8 minutes).

Serves: 2 for main course
Preparation: 15 minutes
Cooking: 5 minutes

"Also delicious with cocktail or sweet and sour sauce!"

— NOTES —

PAELLA VALENCIANA

½	cup olive oil
1	onion (chopped)
1	green pepper (chopped)
½	cup tomatoes (peeled and chopped)
3	cloves garlic (minced)
1	bay leaf
½	lb. pork (cut in chunks)
½	fryer chicken (cut in 4 pieces)
1	lb. lobster (cut in chunks)
½	lb. shrimp (peeled)
8	oysters (shucked)
8	scallops
8	mussels (scrubbed)
4	clams in shells (scrubbed)
4	stone crab claws
1	lb. red snapper (cut in chunks)
3	cups seafood stock, chicken stock or bottled clam juice
	pinch of saffron
1	t. salt
1½	cups rice
¼	cup white wine
1	small can petit green peas (for garnish)
	asparagus (for garnish)
	pimientos (for garnish)

1. Pour olive oil in large heavy casserole. Add onions and peppers and fry until just limp.
2. Add tomatoes, garlic and bay leaf. Cook 5 minutes.
3. Add pork and chicken and sauté until tender, stirring to prevent sticking or burning.
4. Add seafood, stock, saffron, and salt. When this boils, add rice. Stir and bring to second boil.
5. Cover and bake in oven at 350° for 20 minutes.
6. To serve, sprinkle with wine and garnish with peas, asparagus and pimiento.

-continued-

Serves: 4
Preparation: 20-30 minutes
Cooking: 40 minutes
Baking: 20 minutes

"It is an adventure to try this most famous of Spanish dishes! This extremely versatile dish allows you to use almost any native seafood in lieu of the stated ingredients. It is the national dish of Spain."

—NOTES—

Louis PAPPAS

FAMOUS RESTAURANT

In Tarpon Springs, on the banks of the Anclote River, The Louis Pappas restaurant sits in splendor reminding guests of the hanging gardens of Babylon. Its modern cantilevered architecture overflows with green plants, which complement the interior design of hanging baskets and classical Greek sculpture.

Louis Pappas arrived from Sparta, Greece, in 1904 and settled in the Greek community at Tarpon Springs. He and his wife, affectionately known to all as "Mamma", opened the Riverside Cafe in 1925, serving luscious Greek food.

Today, their sons Jack, Mike and Lucas continue the culinary tradition of their ancestors. They invite you to enjoy their hearty Greek cooking seasoned with aromatic spices, while watching sponge boats and pleasure craft nudge their way down the winding Anclote. For the adventurous, they offer such exotic specialties such as *Broiled Octopus* and *Kalamarakia* (baby squid). Their *Stifado* is a delectable beef stew singing with the flavor and rugged character of the sun-drenched Greek Isles. Pappas legendary *Greek Salad* is epic in its proportions, and honey-drizzled *Baklava* will tempt anyone to toss their calorie counter.

While it is not necessary to be as wealthy as the god of Olympus to dine here, possessing a Herculean appetite is often a necessity.

Take U.S. 19 north from Clearwater until it intersects Klosterman Road. Head west on Klosterman to Alternate 19, then take Alternate 19 north into Tarpon Springs. Continue north past St. Nicholas Greek Orthodox Church until Alternate U.S. 19 meets Dodecanese Boulevard. Louis Pappas' famous restaurant is at the corner of Alternate U.S. 19 and Dodecanese Boulevard.

LOUIS PAPPAS FAMOUS GREEK SALAD
(Make Potato Salad in Advance)

— SALAD —

1	large head of lettuce
3	cups of potato salad
12	roka leaves (Greek vegetable) or 12 sprigs watercress
2	tomatoes (cut into 6 wedges each)
1	peeled cucumber (cut lengthwise into 8 fingers)
1	avocado pear (peeled and cut into wedges)
4	1 oz. portions of Feta (Greek cheese)
1	green bell pepper (cut into 8 rings)
4	slices of canned cooked beets
4	shrimp (peeled and cooked)
4	anchovy filets
12	black olives (Greek style preferred)
12	med. hot Salonika peppers (purchased in bottles)
4	fancy cut radishes
4	whole green onions
½	cup distilled white vinegar
¼	cup of olive and salad oil
¼	cup salad oil
	oregano (to taste)

— POTATO SALAD —

6	boiling potatoes
2	medium sized onions (chopped) OR
½	cup thinly sliced green onion
¼	cup parsley (chopped)
½	cup salad dressing
	salt

— POTATO SALAD —

1. Boil potatoes in jackets for approx. 30 minutes, or until tender. Drain, cook, peel and slice into a bowl.
2. Add onions and parsley to potatoes and sprinkle with salt.
3. Fold in salad dressing to hold together lightly.
   Yield: 4 cups.

-continued-

— SALAD —

4. Line rim of large platter with lettuce leaves. Place 3 cups of potato salad in center.
5. Cover with remaining lettuce (shredded). Arrange the roka or watercress or top.
6. Place tomato wedges around base of salad, few on top. Place cucumber wedges between tomatoes. Place avocado outside tomatoes and cucumbers.
7. Slices of Feta cheese should be placed on top, with green pepper rings over all.
8. On top of all, place beet slices with a shrimp on each. An anchovy may top each shrimp. The olives, pepper, radishes, and green onions placed as desired.
9. Sprinkle entire salad with the vinegar, then oil. Oregano sprinkled over all. Serve at once!

Serves: 4
Preparation: 20 minutes
Cooking: 30 minutes for potatoes

"A truly immortal dish."

— NOTES —

MOUSSAKA
(Ground Beef With Eggplant)

3	medium sized eggplant
	salt
1	cup salad oil
6	medium sized potatoes
6	T. butter
1½	cup onion (chopped)
2	cloves garlic
2	lbs. ground lean beef
1	T. salt
1	t. pepper
1	T. dried mint
2	T. fresh parsley (chopped)
½	t. cinnamon
4	T. tomato paste
	cream sauce

— CREAM SAUCE —

¼	lb. butter
¾	cup flour
1	qt. milk (warm)
4	slightly beaten eggs
½	t. salt

1. Leaving skin on, slice eggplant into ½" slices. Sprinkle well with salt, and allow to drain for 20 minutes. Wash off salt. Dry eggplant on towel.
2. Heat oil. Fry slices a few at a time.
3. Slice peeled potatoes into ¼" slices. Fry.
4. Sauté chopped onion and garlic in 6T. butter. Add ground beef. Brown 10 minutes.
5. Add salt, pepper, mint, parsley, cinnamon, and tomato paste. Cook uncovered 10 minutes, to reduce liquid. Set aside.

-continued-

— CREAM SAUCE —

6. Melt butter in sauce pan, remove from heat. Stir in flour until smooth.

7. Slowly add milk, stirring constantly.

8. Add mixture to beaten eggs and cook over low heat until thickened.

— TO ASSEMBLE —

9. Arrange one-half of the eggplant in baking dish, top with one-half of the potato slices and one-half of the meat. Repeat. Top evenly with cream sauce and bake at 375° for 30 minutes or until sauce is set.

Serves: 6-8
Preparation: 45 minutes
Cooking: 30 minutes

"Delicious Greek classic!"
— NOTES —

STIFADO
(Beef Stew with Onions)

2	lbs. lean stew beef
2	T. olive oil
2	T. butter
1	lb. small onions
¼	cup olive oil
2	T. claret wine
2	T. vinegar
4	T. tomato paste
2	t. salt
½	t. pepper
2	cups hot water
2	T. pickling spice (tied in a bag)
4	cloves unpeeled garlic

1. Heat 2T. oil and butter in skillet and brown stew meat for 10 minutes.
2. Put meat in large pot. Brown whole onions in skillet. Add to meat in pot.
3. In a bowl, combine ¼ cup olive oil, wine, vinegar, tomato paste, salt, pepper, water and garlic. Mix. Pour over meat and onions, placing bag of spices in center of stew.
4. Cover and bring to boil. Reduce to simmer. Cook 2 hours or until tender.
5. The gravy may be thickened with small amounts of flour and water.

Serves: 4
Preparation: 25 minutes
Cooking: 2 hours

"Piquant and spicy. Try this one on a cold winter's night."

naples

When Stanley Pate strides through his restaurant, he looks like he should be hoisting the sails on a seaworthy craft instead of being the owner of a popular Naples restaurant. Pate's red sandy hair and beard give him a nautical air that belies long hours spent in a restaurant. However, he chose to get as close to the water as possible with Pate's at Marker "4" in Naples, in furnishings as well as location.

The restaurant is an island-inspired wooden building resting on pilings overlooking Naples Bay. Guests can indulge in tantalizing *Native Lobster*, *Steak Teriyaki* or luscious *Swordfish* as well as other tempting items while watching the surf, seagulls and sailboats outside their porthole. A Dutch *Cappucino* or *Caribbean Coffee* adds to the relaxing mood. Pate's homestyle *Carrot Cake* and *Key Lime Pie* are house favorites, and a recommended conclusion to your nautical dining adventure.

The decor is reminiscent of old New England, much like Stanley Pate's other restaurant on Cape Cod. An ancient ship's wheel, figureheads, oars, and other maritime memorabilia lend that nautical touch. Hanging baskets and café style chairs lead to relaxed informality in dining. It is this ambience that has contributed to the restaurant's popularity among Floridians and their northern guests.

Take to the sea my friend - if but just for an evening at Pate's.

In Naples, U.S. 41 is also 9th Street South. Take 9th Street South to 5th Avenue South. Go west on 5th Avenue South to 8th Street South. Go south on 8th Street South to 1193, near the Coast Guard Station. Next door is Pate's.

Reservations Suggested.

SHRIMP SCAMPI

— SCAMPI BUTTER —

1-2	cloves garlic (chopped fine)
½	T. shallots (chopped)
1	lemon (ground fine including rind and pulp)
½	t. freeze dried chives
2	dashes Tabasco
1	dash Worcestershire sauce
¼	t. salt
¼	t. white pepper
1/8	T. garlic salt
1	stick butter softened (4 oz.)

— SHRIMP —

6	medium shrimp
½	cup fresh bread crumbs
	sherry

— SCAMPI BUTTER —

1. Process all ingredients in blender or food processor (or chop very fine). Add to softened butter. Cover and refrigerate until ready to use.

— SHRIMP —

2. Lightly bread damp shrimp and place in baking dish. Melt one-third of the scampi butter and pour over shrimp evenly. (Reserve remaining scampi butter for future use!)

3. Bake in hot oven about 475º for 8-10 minutes or until just done. Sprinkle with sherry.

Butter yield: ¾ cup
Preparation: 10 minutes
Cooking: 10 minutes
Individual Serving

"This versatile butter may be used on other fish, escargot or even chicken!"

PATE'S CARROT CAKE

— CARROT CAKE —

2	cups flour
1	cup granulated sugar
1	cup brown sugar
1	t. salt
1	T. baking soda
1	T. baking powder
1	T. cinnamon
1	T. nutmeg
4	eggs (beaten)
1	cup salad oil
2	cups carrots (4-6 grated)

— PATE'S ORANGE FROSTING —

8	oz. cream cheese (softened)
1	lb. confectioners sugar
½	t. vanilla
	grated rind from 1 orange
1	T. orange juice (fresh)

— CARROT CAKE —

1. Preheat oven to 350°.
2. Mix the first eight ingredients well.
3. Add eggs, oil and carrots. Mix.
4. Pour into a well greased and dusted 8-cup bundt pan. Let settle 10 minutes.
5. Bake in pre-heated oven for 50 minutes. Cool before removing from pan.

— FROSTING —

6. Mix all frosting ingredients until smooth. Pour over cake.

"Nice orange flavor in the frosting!"

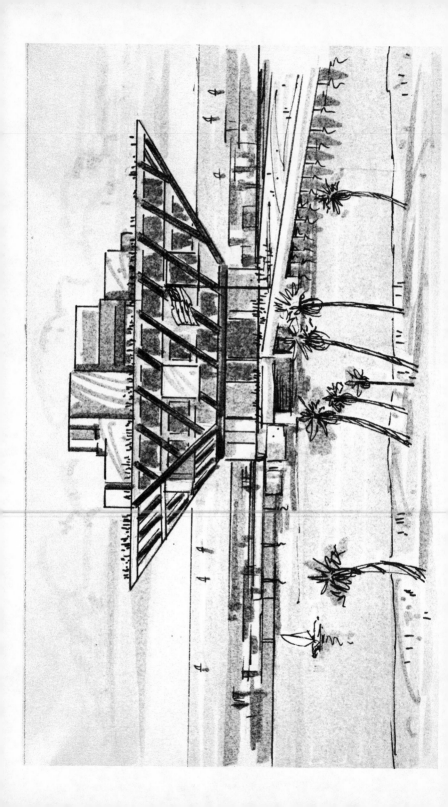

Peter's Place

CAFE INTERNATIONAL

st. petersburg

Sparkling crystal chandeliers punctuate the midnight blue vaulted ceilings. Plush oriental carpets delight the eyes, as well as the weary feet of diners at Peter's Place. Fine silver graces the tables while cane back Breuer chairs add to the pleasure and comfort of continental dining. Restaurateur, Peter Kersker, believes that beauty is enhanced by simplicity, which is clearly reflected in his restaurant's understated elegance and sophistication. Since its opening in 1973, it has been the perfect hideaway for that romantic dinner for two. In the cozy main dining room, spotlessly garbed efficient waiters recite the evening specialties to patrons, while chamber music softly echoes in the background.

The real success of Peter's Place however, is not in the "excellence of the orchestra" but in the orchestrated excellence of exquisite cuisine. The pâté is a subtle whisper upon the palate; the sauces are superb. Peter is passionate in his quest for the very best in dining. He has developed the recipes for his restaurant's multitude of main courses, as well as the ones for such luscious desserts as *Peanut Butter Pie Chantilly*. It is this lovely ambition to excel that has garnered many awards for Peter's Place, and has caused them to be named as one of the top restaurants in Florida by Fodor's.

Peter's Place creates a dining experience to delight the soul, as well as the taste buds. It is, as Peter Kersker advocates, "cuisine as it should be." It should be, and is, marvelous!

Peter's Place is located in St. Petersburg at 208 Beach Drive N.E. Follow Central Avenue east until it intersects Beach Drive. Follow Beach Drive north for almost two blocks. Across the street from the Saint Petersburg Museum of Fine Arts is Peter's Place.

Reservations Suggested.

67

CRÊPE KING CRAB AU SHERRY

1   recipe crêpes*
1   12 oz. pkg. Alaskan king crab, thawed and drained
2   cups medium cream sauce*
1   T. (scant) freeze dried onions
1   T. chives (freeze dried)
1/8   t. nutmeg
2   T. sherry
      dash of salt
      freshly ground pepper to taste
      parsley
      lemon wedge

1. Rinse and drain crabmeat.
2. Prepare white sauce and add onions, chives and nutmeg. Add sherry, salt and pepper. Stir in crabmeat.
3. Spoon mixture into crêpes. Roll and place seam side down in buttered au gratin dish.
4. Bake in 300° oven for 20 minutes or until heated through. Garnish with parsley and lemon wedges.

For variation — Add curry powder, raisins and dry roasted peanuts to crab mixture. Garnish with toasted coconut and chutney on the side.

*See Glossary
Serves: 4
Preparation: 15 minutes
Cooking: 20 minutes

"Delightfully easy!"

FILET MIGNON CORDON BLEU
(Marinate 1 Hour)

— FILETS —

8	filets 1¼" well trimmed
8	very thin slices Swiss cheese
8	thin slices Canadian bacon
	freshly ground pepper
	béarnaise sauce*

— MARINADE —

2	cups red wine
1/3	cup freeze dried chives
½	cup wine vinegar
¼	cup dried onions
1¼	cup sugar
2	T. dried parsley
	salt and pepper

— MARINADE —

1. Combine marinade ingredients and pour over steaks. Marinate 1 hour.

— FILETS —

2. Cut pocket in each steak. Place cheese and bacon in pocket. Close pocket. Grind pepper over each.
3. Broil to desired doneness. Serve warm béarnaise sauce over finished steaks.

*See Glossary
Serves: 8
Preparation: 1 hour/10 minutes
Cooking: 12 minutes

"Sinfully delectible!"

PEANUT BUTTER PIE CHANTILLY

1   9" pie shell baked
¾   cup sugar
1/3 cup flour
2   eggs (beaten)
2   cups milk
1   t. vanilla
2   T. butter
    dash of salt
3   T. crunchy peanut butter
    whipped cream

    dry roasted peanuts
    for sprinkling

1. Mix sugar and flour. Add eggs blending all ingredients well.
2. Stir in milk. Cook over low heat, stirring constantly until mixture thickens.
3. Add vanilla, butter, and salt. Mix well. Stir in peanut butter. Cool slightly.
4. Pour into pie shell and chill.
5. Cover liberally with whipped cream. Sprinkle with chopped, dry roasted peanuts.

Serves: 6-8
Preparation and Cooking: 30 minutes
Chill: 2-3 hours

"This deserves the praise it gets!"

— NOTES —

– NOTES –

the shallows

Mirrors reflect the flickering candlelight and subtly, softly illuminate the four dining rooms of the Shallows. Romance and stimulating aromas fill the air. In fact, the Shallows fulfills the whims and fancies of each of your five senses. This Golden Spoon Award winner is one of Ft. Myers newest and most popular restaurants.

Your entrée choices include common meats and seafoods prepared in quite uncommon, intriguing and delicious ways. The *Breast of Capon Tallyrand* is superb. Chicken has never been dressed so well. Try the *Red Snapper Monte Carlo* or *Veal Oscar*, two house favorites superbly accented with special attire for your occasion. A trip to the circular salad room will bring out the best of one's vegetarian instincts. Heavenly fresh breads are brought to your table by Shallow's "Doughgirl". The *Coconut Bread* is especially moist and fragrant. Breads and sweet rolls are irresistable, but you must save room for the Shallows French pastry cart. It arrives at your table filled with *Cappacciono Cheese Cake, Black Forest Cake, Napoleons* and *Vienna Cream Puffs.* Trés Chic!

Special attention to decorating detail gives this restaurant a perfect "10" for atmosphere. Natural wood, greenery and mirrors lend a fresh outdoors atmosphere while the arrangement of the seating allows for very private moments. It is a very harmonious blend of sophistication and "back to nature". The Shallows may be one of the area's newest but it's certainly "making waves".

At the intersection of U.S. 41 and State Road 865 (also called Gladiolus) just south of Ft. Myers, go west until Gladiolus meets Winkler Road. Go north onto Winkler Road. The Shallows is located at the intersection of Winkler Road and College Parkway.

Reservations Suggested.

SALMON CHARLEMAGNE

4	6-7 oz. salmon fillets
10	oz. white wine
2	t. dill seed
2	t. shallots (minced)
18	oz. medium cream sauce*
	salt, pepper, and garlic to taste
1	small cucumber (thinly sliced)
½	cup flour
½	stick butter
4	oz. mushrooms (sliced and sautéed in butter)
8	strips bacon (cooked crisp)
	lemon wedges and parsley for garnish

1. In a sauce pan, place 8-oz. wine, dill seeds and shallots. Reduce* until almost dry (¼ cup).
2. Make cream sauce. Add dill reduction, 2 remaining oz., wine, salt, pepper and garlic to taste.
3. Add sliced cucumbers to warm dill sauce.
4. Lightly flour and sauté fillets in butter. Bake 350° about 7 minutes.
5. Place on serving platter. Pour sauce over. Sprinkle with sautéed mushroooms. Top with bacon strips. Garnish with lemon and parsley.

*See Glossary
Serves: 4
Preparation: 20 minutes
Cooking: 10 minutes

"This is a lovely cucumber/dill sauce. Does not mask the salmon!"

SNAPPER MONTE CARLO

6	**7 oz. snapper fillets**
6	**oz. mushrooms (sliced)**
6	**oz. scallions (sliced)**
6	**oz. Alaskan snow crabmeat**
	clarified butter*
½	**cup flour for dusting fillets**
	salt, pepper and paprika to taste
12	**oz. béarnaise* sauce**
	lemon wedges and parsley for garnish

1. Sauté mushrooms and scallions in butter. Just before done, add crab. Stir and keep warm.
2. Lightly flour and season fillets with salt, pepper and paprika. Bake at 375º 10-12 minutes or until done.
3. On a plate, place the fillets, topped with a line of mushroom mixture (1/6 for each fillet). Spoon béarnaise over each. Garnish with lemon and parsley.

*See Glossary
Serves: 6
Preparation: 15 minutes
Cooking: 10-12 minutes

"There must be hundreds of ways to prepare Red Snapper. This is one of the best!"

— NOTES —

Siple's Garden Seat

clearwater

Stretch your imagination just a bit. See yourself whizzing down Clearwater's Druid Road in a Stutz Bearcat, accompanied by "swellelegant" ladies and gentlemen, and on your way to an afternoon tea at Siple's Garden Seat. This lovely waterfront restaurant was established in 1920, when Mary Boardman bought the private residence to convert it into a fashionable tea room. Siple's Garden Seat is located in the old Harbor Oaks section of Clearwater, amid ancient Oaks heavy with Spanish Moss, and "Gatsby" style mansions from Florida's boom era of the 1920's. It boasts a magnificent waterfront garden, complete with sparkling white garden seats where in decades gone by, fashionable young ladies in gauzy summer dresses relaxed and enjoyed tea, dainty sandwiches and pastries.

Today, owner Dick Siple, a member of the Chaine des Rotisseurs, carries on the exacting standards for good food set by his Grandmother, Mary Boardman. Siple's Garden Seat has retained its warmth and hospitality with comfortable overstuffed chairs, tiffany lamps, and railings that are actually old brass headboards. Fifteen Florida Trend Golden Spoon Awards are proudly displayed over the fireplace mantle — one for every year the Golden Spoon Award has been presented!

The menu offers continental favorites such as *Shrimp Moutarde* and *Filet Mignon Béarnaise*, as well as popular American favorites such as *Siple's Clam Chowder* and juicy *Standing Rib Roast of Beef.*

Although the original building has undergone a few changes, the fine quality of food and service, as well as the romance of the era, remains the same. Grandmother Boardman would be proud.

Siple's Garden Seat is located at 1234 Druid Road South in Clearwater. Take State Road 60 west to Ft. Harrison Avenue. Go south to Druid Road, then west on Druid, going through the old gateposts marked "Harbor Oaks" and follow the winding road for about one-half mile. Siple's Garden Seat is on the right across from the Morton Plant Hospital. *Reservations Suggested*

CHICKEN BREAST GORGONZOLA

½	stick butter for sautéing (2 oz.)
4	T. minced onions
4	T. sliced fresh mushrooms
4	whole chicken breasts (boned, skinned and flattened, seasoned with salt and fresh ground pepper)
3-4	oz. crumbled Gorgonzola or bleu cheese
6	T. dry white wine
4	T. chicken stock
	roux* or beurre manie for thickening

1. Heat butter. Sauté onions and mushrooms briefly. Remove from pan.
2. Cook chicken breasts on both sides.
3. Add cheese, wine and stock. Thicken with roux only slightly, and return onions and mushrooms to heat through.
4. Serve over rice baked in chicken stock with chopped onion, celery and pimiento.

*See Glossary
Serves: 4
Preparation: 15 minutes
Cooking: 15 minutes

"A notably different way to enjoy Gorgonzola or bleu cheese!"
— NOTES —

-continued-

STRAWBERRIES MARGURITE

32-40 fresh whole strawberries
8   meringue shells (may be ordered from bakery or
      Recipe to follow)

— SAUCE —
1   cup brown sugar (½ lb.)
2   cups sour cream
2   oz. Cointreau liqueur (4T.)
2   oz. Curacao liqueur (4T.)

1.   Wash and hull strawberries.

—SAUCE —
2.   Combine brown sugar, sour cream and liqueurs. Blend
     thoroughly with a wire whisk.
3.   To serve, place 4-5 strawberries around the inside of
     each meringue shell and top with 1/3 cup (3 oz.) of
     sauce.

Serves: 8
Preparation: 10 minutes

"We were enchanted with this dessert! ! !"

— MERINGUE SHELLS —
1   cup sugar (sifted)
3   large egg whites
      dash of salt
½   t. vanilla

1.   Heat sugar and egg whites in small sauce pan until
     approximately 120°. Stir often to prevent burning.
2.   Begin mixing on high speed. Add vanilla and salt. Beat
     until stiff.

-continued-

3. Place meringue in pastry bag with a #3 star tube.
4. Pipe out onto a cookie sheet that has been lined with either silicone or waxed paper. Make a 3" solid circle for the bottom then build up the sides approximately 1-1/2 - 2" in height.
5. Place in a 200° oven at highest point. Bake 1 hour. Shut off heat. Leave shells in oven until thoroughly dry. Place in airtight container until ready to use.

Yield: 6 — 5" shells or 8 — 3" shells
Preparation: 15 minutes
Cooking: 1 hour

"May be made several days in advance . . . surprisingly easy."

— NOTES —

THE RUMACADO

1 oz. peeled ripe avocado
1½ oz. light rum
1½ oz. sweet and sour mix (may be purchased, but best fresh!)
1 T. crushed ice (2-3 cubes)

1. Combine all ingredients in a blender and whirl until smooth and slushy. Serve in cocktail glass.

Serves: 1
Preparation: 5 minutes

"A refreshingly different drink!"

— NOTES —

The Neopolitan, Olde Naples

Truffles
a cafe · Bistro

naples *The Chef's Garden*

Residents of Naples, in southern Florida, will tell you there are three things that make your visit to their beautiful city worthwhile. One is their spectacular beaches, and the others are Truffles and the Chef's Garden.

Truffles is the perfect name for the upstairs eating establishment at 1300 3rd Street South. It's a rare delicacy of a restaurant that features rare delicacies — all this in a casual wooden floor cafe atmosphere. *Cassoulets*, homemade pâtés, terrines, *Cornish Pasties*, and *Ratatouille* highlight the menu with such familiar favorites as *Pastrami & Corned Beef Reubens* and luscious *Smithfield Virginia Ham Sandwiches*.

The Chef's Garden is the more elegant downstairs assemblage for those wishing lunch or supper. Dining room colors are azalea pink and lime green — a perfect foil for the alfresco patio. Like Truffles, the Chef's Garden features the freshest and best available whether it be *Oysters and Artichokes au Gratin* or *Linguine Carbonara*. Owner-chef Tony Ridgway wouldn't have it any other way. He's been cooking and creating gourmet delights since his childhood and is tireless in his efforts to bring the best cuisine to Southwest Florida. Along with his partner, Beirne Brown, Tony constantly creates and changes the menu to insure his guests the ultimate dining experience. Their goal of course, is to keep getting better. Florida Trend Magazine's Golden Spoon Award for three consecutive years testifies to the fact that they must be doing something right at the Chef's Garden — as well as Truffles.

As the poet wrote, "a loaf of bread, a jug of wine and thou." He might also have added Truffles, the Chef's Garden, "and time to savor them both."

Truffles and Chef's Garden are located in the Neapolitan Building in "Olde Naples." In Naples take 9th Street South (Route 41) south to 5th Avenue South. Turn west and go 6 blocks to 3rd Street South. Go south on 3rd Street South to the corner of 3rd Street and 13th Avenue. Truffles and Chef's Garden are on your right at the end of the Neapolitan Building.

Reservations Suggested for dinner at Chef's Garden.

CURRIED MUSSELS
(Allow 6 Hours to Chill)

48	mussels (washed and scrubbed well)
1½	cups water

– SAUCE –

2	T. green onions (minced)
1	T. parsley (minced)
1	t. curry powder
1/8	t. salt
1/8	t. pepper
2	t. lemon juice
2	T. chili sauce
1	T. mussel broth (strained through fine napkin)
1	cup Hellman's mayonnaise

1. Steam mussels in 1½ cups water 8 minutes or until shells open. Remove from shells. Reserve shells and broth.
2. Mix sauce ingredients well. Add well washed (to remove all sand) mussels to sauce. Chill 6 Hours.
3. To serve, spoon mussels and sauce into reserved shells.

Serves: 4 as appetizer
Preparation: 15 minutes
Cook: 8 minutes
Chill: 6 hours

"An interesting sauce that may be used with fish in place of tartar sauce, or as a salad dressing with a curry flavor."

– NOTES –

SHRIMP AND CUCUMBER SOUP
(Allow Time to Chill)

2	cups onion (chopped)
2-3	T. butter
1	qt. chicken stock
1	cup potatoes (peeled and chopped)
½	t. salt
¼	t. pepper
2	small cucumbers or ½ hydroponic cucumber (seed and peel regular cucumber. Wash but do not peel hydroponic).
½	lb. shrimp (cooked, shelled and deveined)
1	cup cream

1. Sauté onion in butter until clear.
2. Add stock and potatoes. Cook until potatoes are tender.
3. Season with salt and pepper. Purée in blender or food processor. Chill.
4. In blender or food processor, coarsely chop shrimp and cucumber. Add to chilled soup. Mix in cream to desired consistency. Taste for seasoning. Serve in frozen cups.

Serves: 6-8
Preparation: 10 minutes
Cooking: 15 minutes
Chill Thoroughly

"Iced soups in Florida are always welcome. This one is especially refreshing!"

— NOTES —

SWEETBREADS WITH LOBSTER

3	lbs. high quality veal sweetbreads
2	1½ lb. lobsters or 1 lb. lobster meat
	juice of 1 lemon
	stock from cooking lobsters
½	stick butter
3	stalks celery (julienne)*
3	carrots (julienne)
8	scallions (julienne)
¼	cup white wine
½	cup crème fraiche*
	salt and pepper to taste

1. Rinse sweetbreads in cold water until it runs clear. Soak in water with lemon juice 30 minutes.
2. Poach sweetbreads in lightly salted water about 5-8 minutes. Place in flat pan and press lightly while chilling.
3. Remove all membrane and tissue. Slice horizontally.
4. Cook lobster in boiling water about 10-12 minutes. Remove meat in large chunks. Reserve stock.
5. Blanche vegetables in boiling water 2 minutes. Put aside.
6. Saute sweetbreads and lobster chunks in butter until heated and browned. Set aside.
7. Add ½ cup lobster stock to pan and de-glaze.* Add wine and cook 2 minutes. Add cream and cook until creamy consistency. Season to taste with salt and pepper.
8. Add vegetables to sauce.
9. Place sweetbreads and lobster on serving platter. Pour sauce over all and serve.

*See Glossary
Serves: 6-8
Preparation: 45 minutes
Cooking: 15/15 minutes

"Light and flavorful!"

– NOTES –

"Old World Charm" is the phrase that most aptly describes The Wine Cellar Restaurant and Cocktail Lounge. Located on Redington Beach, (midway between Clearwater Beach and the southern-most tip of St. Petersburg Beach), it has been an overwhelming success with area residents and visitors alike. The Wine Cellar has also been a consistent award winner. Among the most recent have been the Mobil Guide Four Star Award, Tampa Bay Life Magazine's Silver Plate Award, and the Florida Trend Magazine's Golden Spoon Award. Owner-chefs Ted Sonnenschein, Peter Schuckert, and Karl Klumpp diligently maintain the high standards their restaurant is noted for. Ted is one of the few area members of the international *Chaine des Rotisseurs* — the "Rolls Royce" of culinary organizations.

Dining at the Wine Cellar is a holiday in Europe, at a fraction of the expense. A comfortable Old World atmosphere surrounds you regardless of which country you visit. The Italian Room, Spanish Room, French Room, Swiss Room, and The Wine Cellar will take you on a European tour filled with authentic charm. In a more romantic light, there is even a European "Street" room, with little café tables amongst brick store fronts with warmly lighted shop windows.

The menu boasts of such succulent entrées as *Froglegs Provençale* and *Chateaubriand Bouquetiere*, eleven sinfully rich desserts and twelve different specialty coffees. The ample winelist includes a *Chateau Lafitte Rothschild 1967*, secluded as a prized possession would be, in the Wine Cellar's "winecellar". Nothing is overlooked by the watchful eyes of Ted, Peter, and Karl in their quest to provide you with a unique dining experience. As the menu states: "Our greatest reward is taking pride in making your visit to the Wine Cellar a happy and memorable one". And, for me, the Wine Cellar will long be remembered as one of my favorite travel adventures.

The Wine Cellar is on North Redington Beach at 17307 Gulf Boulevard. Reservations Suggested.

COCONUT FRIED SHRIMP

2	lbs. shrimp (uncooked)
1¼	cups flour
½	T. double action baking powder
½	T. salt
1	cup milk
1	whole egg
3	T. melted butter
	long shredded coconut

1. Shell and devein shrimp, leaving tail on. Split shrimp without separating.
2. Sift flour with baking powder and salt; adding milk, egg and melted butter to make batter. Beat well.
3. Dip each shrimp in batter, holding by tail and let excess drain off.
4. Roll in shredded coconut and deep fry at 375° until golden. Serve immediately.

Serves: 6-8
Preparation: 30 minutes
Cooking: 10-15 minutes total, for frying a few at a time.

"Irresistible first course or appetizer! !"

— NOTES —

TED'S SWISS CHEESE SOUP

1	T. butter
½	cup + 2T. flour
1	cup + 4T. chicken stock
2½	cups + 2T. milk
8	oz. Kraft's Cheese Whiz
8	oz. Swiss cheese, shredded
	salt
	white pepper
1	cup + 4T. sauterne wine (10 oz.)
3	oz. Kirschwasser (6T.)

1. Melt butter in sauce pan. Slowly add flour to make roux.
2. Add chicken stock and milk, stirring constantly. Bring to a boil and let simmer for 15 minutes.
3. Stir in Cheese Whiz and Swiss cheese. Stirring constantly, simmer for an additional 5 minutes.
4. Add salt and pepper and correct seasoning.
5. Just before serving, add sauterne wine and let simmer for and additional minute.
6. After dishing out in soup cups, put a small dash of Kirschwasser on top of each serving.

Serves: 10

Preparation and cooking: 35 minutes

"Always a hit! !"

— NOTES —

BONELESS BREAST OF CHICKEN AND
LOBSTER au GRAND MARNIER
(Allow Time to Marinate Overnight)

4   chicken breasts (skinned, boned and gently flattened, must be double breasted). Marinate overnight in 1 cup of orange juice.

4   3 oz. African lobster tails (poached in water with 1 sliced lemon, cooled and removed whole from shells).

2   t. Grand Marnier
     salt and pepper
     Lea and Perrins Worcestershire sauce

1   stick of butter (4 oz.)
     paprika

1   bunch parsley (chopped)

3   oz. toasted sliced almonds (for garnish)
     orange sections (for garnish)

— SAUCE GRAND MARNIER —

2   cups chicken sauce*
     juice of 1 orange

4   T. butter

4   T. Grand Marnier

— CHICKEN —

1.   Put marinated chicken breasts on flat surface and brush with 2T. melted butter. Sprinkle with salt, pepper, Lea and Perrins sauce, chopped parsley and Grand Marnier.

2.   Place lobster tail in center of chicken breast and fold chicken firmly over tail. Turn over and place in baking pan. Brush top of each with 4T more of melted butter. Dash with paprika.

3.   Bake at 375° for 25 minutes. DO NOT OVERCOOK.

*to drippings from baked chicken breasts, add enough chicken stock to measure 2 cups of chicken sauce.

-continued-

— SAUCE GRAND MARNIER —

4. Take 2 cups chicken sauce, bring to boil, stir in juice of 1 orange and 4T. butter. May be thickened with corn-starch mixed with a little stock. Taste for salt. Put aside.

5. Place remaining Grand Marnier in a small pan and warm (please warm only). Light carefully and pour while flaming into chicken sauce.

6. To serve, glaze chicken breast with Sauce Grand Marnier and sprinkle with sliced almonds. Garnish with orange sections. Serve remaining sauce on side.

Serves: 4
Preparation: After marinating overnight, 30-40 minutes.
Cooking: 30/10 minutes

"This recipe was the award winner in the Grand Marnier sponsored contest in Chicago for Hilton chefs in 1965. Truly elegant dining!"

— NOTES —

boynton beach

Bernard's is a slightly smaller version of a tile-roofed turreted castle from the Spanish countryside, surrounded by dense tropical foliage. The building was originally designed in 1929 as headquarters for the then famous Rainbow Tropical Gardens, created by the renown horticultural expert C.O. Miller. In the early days, the gardens were an important tourist attraction and a claim to fame for the town of Boynton Beach. A hurricane in 1947 decimated The Gardens. However, the architecturally sound building lost only a few roof tiles. Today, the building shines like a little beacon through the dense underbrush which surrounds it.

The tropical mood is carried throughout the restaurant with cane and bamboo chairs, floral prints, potted plants and muted earth tones. Exposed beam ceilings rise above the rough stucco walls. A favorite dining room has a covered patio area with stark white corinthian columns, ceiling fans, and wicker chairs. Brass table appointments, hurricane lamps and plates gleam on the crisp white tablecloths. French doors open out onto the dining patio under beveled glass in a *fleur-de-lis* design.

The *fleur-de-lis* design is present for good reason. The owners are Jacques Graf and Chef John Faure. They're responsible for the continental accent in the American and Island cuisine here at Bernard's. A *New York Sirloin Steak* finds true happiness with a *Bahamian Conch Chowder*. *Escargots de Bourgogne* make an excellent marriage with the

Fillet of Fresh Grouper, Peas and Rice Plantain. (Plantain is a tropical banana-like fruit often enjoyed by Islanders.) *Roast Long Island Duckling Hawaiian* sings of paradise. Bernard's specialties such as *Steak Au Poivre* draw rave reviews and the *Conch Chowder* recipe was requested so often that little cards containing the recipe were printed up to give to guests. Rumor has it that no one is a true Floridian until he has tasted Conch Chowder and Key Lime Pie!

Bernard's . . . a taste of the islands in a setting so serene. What more could we ask?

In Boynton Beach take the N.W. 2nd Avenue exit east from I-95. Keep going east to Route 1, which is also N. Federal Highway. Go north on North Federal to 1730. Bernard's is on the right.

Reservations Suggested.

BAHAMIAN CONCH CHOWDER

6	cleaned conch (ground or chopped clams)
1	large carrot (diced)
1	green pepper (diced)
2	onions (diced)
½	stick butter
½	t. thyme
½	t. oregano
	salt and pepper to taste
1	can whole tomatoes (1 lb. 13 oz.)
½	can tomato paste (freeze remaining in 1T. portions for future use)
1	qt. of fish stock/court bouillon*
3	T. flour
4	T. butter
6	T. sherry

1. Saute´conch , carrot, green pepper and onion in butter.
2. Add thyme, oregano, salt, pepper, tomatoes and tomato paste. Stir in stock.
3. Bring to boil for a few minutes. Simmer for ½ hour.
4. Brown flour, mix in butter. Add a little stock from hot chowder and return mixture to chowder. Continue to simmer until ready to serve.
5. To serve, add a 1T. sherry to each bowl. Ladle in chowder.

*See Glossary
Serves: 6
Preparation: 10 minutes
Cooking: 45 minutes

"A famous recipe that always pleases!"

CHICKEN CHASSEUR

6	chicken breasts (or preferred pieces to serve 6)
	flour
	salt and pepper to taste
	butter for sautéing
1	cup onion (chopped)
1	clove garlic (minced)
3	oz. butter
½	lb. bacon (diced)
½	lb. mushrooms (sliced)
1	qt. beef consommé
1 1/3	cup white wine
1	T. cornstarch mixed with 1T. water
¼	cup parsley (chopped)
1	t. Worcestershire
	dash of Tabasco
1/8	cup brandy

1. Flour, salt and pepper chicken. Saute until golden brown.
2. Sauté onions, garlic in butter. Add bacon and brown. Add mushrooms. Simmer 15 minutes.
3. Add consommé, wine. Bring to boil. Add chicken and simmer 1 hour.
4. Thicken sauce with cornstarch mixture. Add parsley, Worcestershire, Tabasco and brandy. Taste for salt and pepper. Serve.

Serves: 6
Preparation: 20 minutes
Cooking: 20/1 hour

"A blissful combination of flavors!"

ROAST TENDERLOIN OF BEEF HENRI IV

3   lb. tenderloin (trimmed of fat and tissue)
¼   cup butter
2   cups beef bouillon
    cornstarch
6   artichoke bottoms
    béarnaise sauce

— BÉARNAISE SAUCE —
½   cup white wine
1   T. tarragon leaves
2   T. red wine vinegar
3   T. shallots (minced)
1   sprig thyme or ¼ t. dry
5   egg yolks (beaten)
12   oz. butter (melted)
    salt, white pepper
    Accent to taste
    juice of 1 lemon
1/3   cup parsley chopped

1.   Roast tenderloin in butter in hot oven 400° - 450° for 20 minutes. Remove from pan. Make a gravy with bouillon, drippings and a little cornstarch. Serve with roast.

— BÉARNAISE SAUCE —
2.   While roast is cooking, combine wine, tarragon, vinegar, shallots and thyme in a sauce pan. Cook and reduce* to 1/3.
3.   Add egg yolks, stirring constantly with a whisk. (About 4 minutes.)
4.   Remove from heat and slowly add butter, whipping with whisk until consistency of whipped cream.

    *See Glossary   -continued-

5. Season with salt, white pepper, Accent and lemon juice. Keep warm.

6. To serve, surround roast with artichoke bottoms filled with béarnaise sauce. Serve extra sauce on side.

Serves: 6
Preparation: 10 minutes
Cooking: 20/15 minutes

"This may turn out to be your béarnaise forever. It is certainly an excellent one!!"

— NOTES —

The Breakers, Palm Beach

Palm Beach, Florida

The Breakers. The name suggests mystery, intrigue, grandeur. Images of palaces and grand hotels of Europe crowd the mind. It is the *super-ultimate* in a city where the ultimate is strictly "de rigeuer." Palm Beach is the Palm Springs of the South on a slightly smaller scale, but none the less magnificent. Perhaps the single intrusion of crime in the town's exclusive streets is a Rolls Royce Silver Cloud, parked beyond its time limit.

Enter the stately tree-lined avenue and catch the first glimpse of this regal beauty, adorned with the magnificent twin towers. The Breakers is certainly the Grande Dame of hotels. Built in 1925, it is the third hotel structure to occupy the grounds. In the early 1900's, Henry Morrison Flagler of the prominent Flagler family, built the Palm Beach Inn on the site. The Inn was later replaced by a more elaborate structure that he named The Breakers. A raging fire destroyed the original wooden structure of The Breakers in 1925. In a record-breaking 11½ months, the Flagler heirs had a new hotel built at a cost of six million dollars.

Architect Leonard Schultze, well-known for his designs of the Waldorf-Astoria in New York, had taken his artistic inspiration from the most fabulous villas in Italy. The Villa Medici in Rome is seen in The Breakers twin belvedere towers and graceful arches. The Florentine fountain, directly in front of the hotel, is patterned after one in the Bobli Gardens in Florence. The lobby with its vaulted ceilings and dazzling frescos causes instant hyperventilation by its magnificence, and suggests the ceiling of the Sistine chapel or the

THE BREAKERS

Palazzo Carega in Genoa. The central courtyard is similar to the inner gardens of the Villa Sante in Rome. And to the east is the Mediterranean Ballroom which takes its inspiration from the Palazzo Deg'l Imperial at Genoa.

Elaborate ceilings, Renaissance portraits, colossal tapestries, a Venetian chandelier of bronze, mirrors and crystals, delicate antiques, incredible grandeur, and flamboyant richness — all recall the Mediterranean heritage of Florida. From the first footprints of the Conquistadors to the feathered tread of a Gucci loafer, The Breakers unfolds the story of the romantic land that is Florida, in a setting where time is measured from shimmering sunset to sunset and the most complicated cares are "When do we tee off?" and "Tennis anyone?"

Architecture and decor are not the only features of this hotel that are done on a grand scale. Executive Chef Manfred Hacker supervises a staff of over 200 and changes the menu on a daily basis so there will be no possibility for boredom to set in among long term guests. Formerly with the Omni International Hotels in Atlanta, Hacker brings his culinary expertise to such gourmet favorites at *Filet of Beef Wellington Bordelaise*, *Mocha Mousse* and *Breast of Chicken Veronique*.

Just imagine relaxing in one of the palatial Florentine rooms, nibbling on *Quiche Lorraine* or sipping *Mouton Cadet*, when in walks your favorite movie star or a top fashion model! It happens at The Breakers — that castle by the sea, by the beautiful sea.

To find The Breakers, just get behind the nearest Rolls Royce heading east from I-95 on the Southern Boulevard exit. Go all the way east to the beach on Southern Boulevard, then take County Road north to 1 County Road, and that's The Breakers!

Reservations Suggested.

FILET OF BEEF MANFRED

— FOR EACH SERVING —

1   7 oz. filet
      salt and pepper to taste
1   t. olive oil
1   t. shallots (minced)
2   fresh tomatoes (peeled and chopped)
1   t. capers (chopped)
2   oz. puff pastry (may be purchased in frozen food sec-
      tion of supermarket, Pepperidge Farm brand)
1   thin slice Prosciutto or ham
1   egg (beaten)
      béarnaise sauce

1. Salt and pepper filet. Brown both sides in olive oil in hot skillet, quickly so as not to cook. Cool in refrigerator.
2. Add shallots to the oil. Sauté 1 minute. Add tomatoes and capers. Sauté 10 minutes. Cool.
3. Roll puff pastry into very thin square. Place one-half of the tomato mixture in center. Top with cold filet and the remaining half of the tomato mixture. Wrap ham over top.
4. Brush egg around exposed pastry. Bring opposite corners over the filet and press together. Seal to make attractive package. Decorate with excess pastry.
5. Bake in hot oven 350° - 400° for 25 minutes. (Can be prepared in morning and refrigerated until time to bake.) Serve with béarnaise sauce*.

*See Glossary
Serves: 1
Preparation: 20 minutes
Bake: 25 minutes

"To serve this entrée is to impress and delight your guests. Step by step, it is easy to create!"

RACK OF LAMB BREAKERS
(Start Sauce Several Hours Ahead)

1	double rack of lamb (about 5 lbs.)
1	t. olive oil
2	t. shallots (chopped)
1	lb. mushrooms (ground)
¼	t. tarragon
1	t. fresh parsley
2	cloves garlic (minced)
¼	t. tarragon mustard
¼	t. fresh ground pepper
8	oz. puff pastry (may be purchased in frozen food section, Pepperidge Farm brand)
2	eggs (beaten)

— LAMB SAUCE —

1	carrot (cut)
1	onion (cut)
1	stalk celery (cut)
1	clove garlic
1	T. tomato paste
1	cup fresh mint (chopped)
¼	cup dry mint
2	T. vinegar
1	t. sugar
	salt and pepper to taste
	lamb bones

1. Carefully remove the eye of the rack (tenderloin). Refrigerate.
2. Cut all meat from bones (reserve bones). Cut ALL fat from meat. Discard fat.
3. Grind the extra meat (not the eye).

— LAMB SAUCE —
4. Brown lamb bones, carrot, onion, celery and garlic under broiler.

-continued-

5. Place in large pot. Add water to cover. Add 1T. tomato paste. Simmer/boil 2 hours until reduced to 2-3 cups. Strain.
6. Add mint, vinegar, sugar, salt and pepper. Simmer. Taste for seasonings. (Yield: 2 cups).
7. In a hot skillet, sauté the shallots in oil for 2 minutes. Add mushrooms 2-3 minutes. Add ground meat, constantly stirring. Add tarragon, parsley, garlic. Stir. Remove from heat. Cool.
8. Brush mustard on cool eye of rack. Sprinkle with pepper. Add few drops of olive oil to pan and brown eye fast on all sides for about 5 minutes. Refrigerate immediately.
9. Add 1 egg to cool mushroom-meat mixture.
10. Roll out pastry to 1/8" thick and place on baking sheet. Put cool eye in center. Pat mushroom mixture over eye. Fold pastry over all and seal. Decorate the masterpiece with remaining pastry. (May be prepared in advance at this point.)
11. When ready to cook, brush pastry with remaining egg. Bake in 350° - 400° oven 20-25 minutes. Let sit 5 minutes. Slice. Serve with lamb sauce on side.

Serves: 4
Preparation: 20 minutes
Cooking: 2 hours/40 minutes

"This recipe is written step-by-step in order to duplicate this chef's fine recipe. At first glance, it seems more difficult than it really is. At any rate, it is worth every effort. Indulge yourself!"

THYBEN SALMON
(Allow 48 Hours to Pickle and Dry)

1	lb. salmon fillet (skin on)
3½	oz. pickling salt (may be found in Gourmet Specialty Shops)
1	t. sugar
1	bay leaf
½	t. white pepper (fresh ground)
½	t. all spice
4	juniper berries (crushed)
1	t. coriander
½	t. mustard seed
1	cup onions (diced)
½	cup celery (diced)
½	cup carrots (diced)
1	bunch dill (chopped)
1	bunch parsley (chopped)

— SAUCE —

1	t. mustard
1	egg yolk
1	t. white wine vinegar
2	t. simple syrup
¾	cup oil
1	t. marinade mixture
	chopped dill

1. Cover salmon completely with pickling salt.
2. Cover evenly with the spices.
3. Add onions, celery and carrots to cover.
4. Sprinkle all over with dill and parsley.
5. Place covered in refrigerator 24 hours.
6. Brush off marinade ingredients and dry 24 hours in refrigerator. Should retain red color. Slice thin to serve with sauce.

-continued-

— SAUCE —

7. In a blender or food processor, blend first 4 ingredients. Add oil VERY slowly (drop by drop), as you would a mayonnaise. Add marinade and dill. Mix and chill well.

Serves: 4 as appetizer
Preparation: 15 minutes
Pickling time: 48 hours

"This looks so attractive while being prepared and smells even better. Wait until you taste it!"

— NOTES —

CASA VECCHIA

It may be a "casa vecchia", but it is certainly one "old house" everyone would love to have as their very own. Opened in 1979 by the team of Leonce Picot and Al Kocab, this exquisite little house is a tribute to Northern Italian cuisine in a setting of unparalleled elegance, in one of the finest areas of Fort Lauderdale.

The Casa Vecchia was built as a private residence on the Intracoastal Waterway in 1938 by an heir to the Pond's Cold Cream fortune. Years of neglect took its toll before the house was purchased in the late 1970's by Picot and restored to its original elegance. With the addition of carefully chosen furnishings and the characteristic Picot attention to detail, patrons know they are going to partake of a very sensuous dining experience. The intimate atmosphere of the Casa Vecchia is quite unlike that of the average restaurant. One feels he or she is sharing a meal with the lord of the manor in his elegant villa.

Furnishings of timeless beauty are in lavish abundance. Intricate Victorian, flamboyant art nouveau, fussy Italian Provincial. One of the rooms is like an Italian parlour at the turn of the century with lush "cabbage rose" style carpeting and an ornate Viennese clock. Vibrant tile tables in the greenhouse room display the Baccarat crystal and ethereal Villeroy et Boch china. Lush palms and Florida foliage are everywhere and fresh imported flowers perfume the air. Diners on the al fresco patio can listen to the lapping of the waves in rhythm with lights dancing along on the waterfront.

The Casa Vecchia is a dining event, from the *Carpaccio*, paper thin slices of raw beef with a piquant mayonnaise, to the homemade ice creams and sorbets. In what other restaurant could be found a divine and perfectly blended *Capellini O Linguine All Carbonara* with homemade pasta, or *Côte´de Porc Farcie des Gourmets*, pork loin chops made with herbs grown in the herb garden just a few feet away from the kitchen? Attention to the most minute detail is evidenced throughout — even the butter is adorned with a delicate crowning of parsley leaf for beauty. Lamb, quail, "bistecca" and an abundance of seafood complete a menu noted for its fresh, quality food. Add to this an extensive wine list featuring the best in French, Californian, Italian, German and Spanish wines — pure heaven!

This quest to present the utmost in dining has made Casa Vecchia a winner of the Mobil Four Star Award and Travel/Holiday Magazine Award.

From the ordered pathways of the formal garden, to the paper thin long stemmed crystal wine glasses, Casa Vecchia is a restaurant to be savored and experienced again and again. Multo Bené!

Casa Vecchia is located at 209 North Birch Road in Fort Lauderdale. Take the Sunrise Blvd. exit from I-95 and go east toward the beach. When Sunrise Blvd. ends, take A1A south to Alhambra. Then go west on Alhambra, which "dead ends" into Birch Road and Casa Vecchia.

Reservations Suggested.

LUMACHE ALLA CASALINGA
(Snails in Phyllo Pastry)

3	dozen snails
6	cloves garlic (minced)
1	t. olive oil
1	cup tomato sauce
	salt and pepper to taste
½	lb. spinach (cooked and drained)
	salt, pepper and nutmeg to taste
1	t. olive oil
3	sheets Phyllo Pastry dough (available in Greek or Lebanese Bakeries)
1	egg
1½	cup brown sauce*
1	t. oregano

1. In a skillet lightly sauté garlic in 1 t. olive oil. DO NOT BROWN. Add snails and stir for 2 minutes.
2. Add tomato sauce, salt and pepper. Cook 3 minutes. Set aside and cool in refrigerator.
3. Season spinach with salt, pepper and nutmeg. Mix in 1 t. olive oil.
4. Cut each Phyllo sheet in half lengthwise (into 2 long strips).
5. On one end of each strip make a bed of spinach (3" X 1½" X 1¼" thick.)
6. Place 6 snails on each bed and roll jelly-roll fashion. Seal ends with beaten egg. Bake 20 minutes at 350º.
7. Boil brown sauce with oregano for 2 minutes.
8. To serve, place 2 T. brown sauce on each of 6 plates. Top with baked snails in Phyllo roll.

*See Glossary

Serves: 6
Preparation: 15 minutes
Chill: 2 hours
Bake: 20 minutes

"Cut through this light flaky pastry and discover a nice surprise. . . escargot with a superb flavor!"

TROTA ALLA PRIMAVERA
(Trout Primavera)

2	fresh trout/12-14 oz. each (cut in fillets)
	milk (for dipping)
¼	lb. butter
2	carrots (julienne*)
1	zucchini (julienne)
	handful of snow pea pods (julienne)
1	green pepper (julienne)
1	can pimientos (julienne)
1	small onion (julienne)
2	celery stalks (julienne)
2	T. fresh basil or ½ t. dry (opt.)
	salt and pepper to taste
2	cups hollandaise sauce*
1	cup whipping cream

1. Melt butter in large skillet. Add vegetables in order of cooking time (i.e. carrots first). Sauté until cooked but still crunchy (5 mins.). Season and put aside.
2. Dip fish fillets in milk, dust with flour and sauté on both sides. Place in baking dish. Top with vegetables. (May be prepared 1 day in advance at this point and refrigerated.)
3. Mix hollandaise with whipping cream to make a mousseline sauce*. Keep warm.
4. Heat trout and vegetables in mod. oven 325°. Serve with mousseline sauce over top.

*See Glossary
Serves: 2-3
Preparation: 15 minutes
Cooking: 10/5 minutes

"A beautiful and colorful dish. The trout is excellent. We also tried it with grouper!"

SPUMA DI CIOCCOLATA
(Allow Time To Freeze)

3 egg yolks
1 cup sugar
2 oz. Marsala
1 pt. whipping cream
¼ cup black raisins

1. In a sauce pan, cream together eggs and sugar. Heat until thick.
2. Add 1-oz. Marsala.
3. Whip cream, add to above, add remaining Marsala and raisins until blended.
4. Pour into sherbet cups and freeze.

Serves: 6
Preparation: 15 minutes
Freeze: 4 hours

"Make days in advance. It's a dessert and an after-dinner drink all in one! !"

— NOTES —

palm beach

Down a palm-lined street in Palm Beach on the main floor of the Plaza Center is the favorite gathering place of Palm Beach's young executives — Chez Guido. The "Guido" in the restaurant's name is the Swiss-born and trained owner, Guido Gerosa. He and his lovely wife are the ever-present host and hostess of Chez Guido constantly evidencing their care and concern, and stopping to greet diners with welcome smiles and lighthearted conversation.

Continental favorites such as *Steak A La Russe* can be enjoyed in the cheery garden-like dining room called "Chez Guido South". The decor is vibrant with spring greens and pale lemon yellows. Plants and mint green window treatments enhance the lively mood. Paintings are displayed in art gallery fashion along the walls. "Chez Guido North" has more of an earth-toned warm brick pub atmosphere.

Whichever room Palm "Beachers" choose, they can be sure that Guido's "garden" will bloom with perennial favorites. Begin with the pâté maison. It's an eye-catching arrangement graced by toast points, lettuce, tomato, egg and parsley. The *Fresh Trout* is really fresh and delicious. There's the popular and zesty *Bouillabaisse* along with other seafood enticements. *Veal Chops* are also an excellent choice.

Chez Guido. It's relaxing, friendly and a charming reflection of the character of its owners.

To find Chez Guido, take the Okeechobee exit east off I-95 and go east. That's going to be Royal Palm Way after the bridge. Chez Guido is located in the first office building at the left side after the school playground.

Reservations Suggested.

BOUILLABAISSE

2	onions (chopped)
1	leek (chopped)
2	tomatoes (chopped)
2	cloves garlic (minced)
2	T. parsley (chopped)
1	bay leaf
½	t. thyme
2	strands of saffron
½	cup oil
2	qt. fish stock*
	salt and pepper to taste
1	lb. swordfish (cubed)
1	lb. grouper (cubed)
8	shrimp
8	clams
16	mussels
4	small lobster tails (cut in half)

1. Sauté the first nine ingredients in oil for 5 minutes. Add the stock, salt and pepper. Simmer 20 minutes.
2. Add the seafood. Cook 15 minutes.
3. Remove the fish to a large casserole. Reduce* the stock for 3 minutes. Taste for seasoning and pour over fish.

*See Glossary
Serves: 8
Preparation: 20 minutes
Cooking: 45 minutes

"A hearty soup with great seafood flavor! !"

STEAK À LA RUSSE

— FOR EACH SERVING —

7	oz. fillet (¼" thick)
1	t. butter
1	T. vodka
1	shallot (chopped)
3	oz. mushrooms (sliced)
1	t. Dijon mustard
1	t. Worcestershire sauce
½	cup red wine sauce*
¼	cup heavy cream
1	T. vodka
2	T. sour cream (room temperature)
	salt and fresh ground pepper to taste

1. In a very hot sauté pan, add butter. Cook fillet on both sides until desired doneness. Flame with vodka. Remove to warm plate.
2. Sauté shallots and mushrooms. Add mustard, Worcestershire and red wine sauce. Blend well.
3. Add heavy cream, 1T. vodka, stirring. Add sour cream, salt and pepper. Pour over steak and serve with wild rice.

*Note:
    To make red wine sauce add:
1   cup red wine to
1   cup brown* sauce
    Reduce to ½ cup.

 *See Glossary
Serves: 1
Preparation: 5 minutes
Cooking: 20 minutes

"Treat yourself with this unique steak recipe!"

Christine Lee's
NORTHGATE

ft. lauderdale

For Chinese food, Christine Lee's Northgate Restaurant in Fort Lauderdale is the ultimate in Oriental elegance. Critically acclaimed as Florida's "Best Chinese Restaurant", this pearl of the Orient features the uncommon Szechwan and Mandarin style of cuisine, as well as the popular Cantonese style. However, there's nothing common about Christine Lee's — you won't see artificial plastic dragons, "red on everything" decor, or placemates describing your personality traits based on your year of birth. What you will see is generous, gracious hospitality, and Oriental simplicity in its purest form.

Wicker chairs, natural wood accents, plants, attractive custom designed wall murals and subdued lighting lend a feeling of sophistication. Service is continental style with frequent clearing of the table for the next course — allowing for uncluttered and relaxed dining. Efficient, well trained waiters helpfully caution novices concerning the spicyness of such entrees as *Sauteed Prawn Szechwan Style*. That hot sauce is really a four-alarmer! The fresh, crisp eggrolls are unlike any you have ever tasted, unless you have gone to the great effort of making them yourself. Classic favorites such as *Lobster Cantonese* and *Peking Duck* appear on the menu side by side with *King Size Sirloin Steak*, a lusciously tender *Filet Mignon* and *Double Cut Loin Lamb Chops*. For dessert your waiter might suggest the *Peach Melba*, *Pear Helene*, or perhaps the unbelievably rich *Chocolate-chocolate* ice cream. Of course whether you have room for dessert or not, you'll enjoy the tradition of breaking a delicate fortune cookie to celebrate the conclusion of a good meal and read of the good things in your future.

And yes, there really is a Christine Lee. This gracious and vivacious woman is a native of Taiwan. Christine came to the United States in 1953 knowing little about the restaurant business. She went to work in Chinese restaurants in San Francisco and later New York. Her intelligence and drive have made her a success. Now, she and her family have two restaurants in Florida with plans to open others. With the assistance of her husband Steve Mallock, her lovely daughter Mary and son-in-law Lucky Carothers, and the encouragement of her family and friends, she will certainly succeed.

Christine Lee's Northgate is where East meets West in a most happy marriage. It's a rare restaurant, very well done!

To find Christine Lee's Northgate, take I-95 to Commercial Blvd. exit in Fort Lauderdale. Go west on Commercial Blvd. for at least five miles, past 441, over the Florida Turnpike to Rock Island Road. Go north on Rock Island Road to 6191. Christine Lee's is on the left side flanked by condominiums.

Reservations Suggested.

CHINESE FRIED DUMPLINGS

— DOUGH —

May purchase 3" round wrappers at Oriental grocers or make with the following ingredients:

3½ cups flour (1 lb.)
1¼ cups water

— STUFFING —

1   lb. lean ground pork
½   cup Chinese cabbage (chopped fine)
1   t. fresh ginger (minced)
1   cup chicken broth
1   T. dry sherry
½   t. white pepper
2   t. salt

— SAUCE —

½   cup Kikkoman soy sauce
1   T. vinegar
1   t. chili paste (optional - may be purchase at Oriental grocers)

— TO MAKE DOUGH —

1. Mix flour and water in mixer, beat until smooth. Cover with wet towel and refrigerate 3 hours.
2. Roll dough to 1" thick. Shape in round roll. Slice in ½" pieces. Roll piece into 3" rounds.

— TO MAKE STUFFING —

3. Mix all ingredients thoroughly and refrigerate 3 hours.
4. Place 2 t. stuffing in center of each dough round. Crimp edges to seal.
5. Drop dumplings in boiling water, stirring to prevent sticking. Boil each batch 10 minutes. Drain very well.

-continued-

6. The dumplings may be served at this point with a sauce (or in clear broth with chopped green onion, Bok Choy-Chinese Cabbage and shredded cooked meat).
7. For appetizers, fry carefully on one side in small amount of oil (1T.). Dip in sauce.

— SAUCE —
8. Blend well.

Yield: About 75/100 dumplings

"These delicately seasoned dumplings may be made in advance and frozen! !"

— NOTES —

NEPTUNE'S DELIGHT

8	large shrimp (peeled, deveined and butterflied)
½	lb. sole fillet (cut in 1" slices)
1	cup scallops (cleaned)
3	t. cornstarch
2	egg whites
3	cups peanut oil
2	stalks broccoli (cut in 3" long pieces)
½	cup straw mushrooms (available at Oriental markets)
½	cup water chestnuts (sliced)
½	cup baby corn (available in Gourmet Specialty Shops or Oriental markets)
2	stalks celery (cut in thirds)
¼	cup scallions (chopped)
½	t. fresh ginger, (minced)
2	drops sesame oil (available at Oriental markets)

— SAUCE —

1	cup chicken broth
1	T. wine
½	t. sugar
½	t. salt/dash pepper
1	T. cornstarch
½	t. M.S.G. (optional)

— SAUCE —
1. Mix sauce ingredients well. Set aside.

— SEAFOOD —
2. Mix each seafood separately with 1t. cornstarch and 1/3 of the egg whites and ½ t. oil.
3. Heat oil in wok or heavy deep skillet to very hot. Drop sole in piece by piece. Cook 1 minute. Add scallops, cook ½ minute. Add shrimp, cook 1 minute more. Scoop out and drain.
4. Heat oil again. Add broccoli. Cook 1 minute. Add mushrooms, chestnuts and corn. Scoop out and drain.

5. Remove oil from wok. Return 1 T. Heat, stir in scallions, ginger for few seconds. Add seafood and vegetables. Pour in well mixed sauce. Heat ½ minute. Add 2 drops sesame oil. Serve with white rice.

Serves: 4
Preparation: 20 minutes
Cooking: 10 minutes

"One of the joys of fine Chinese food is the subtle flavor of chosen ingredients and their sauces, requiring no addition of Soy. This is one of those dishes! !"

— NOTES —

The Down Under is not a restaurant that features Australian cuisine. It is an adorable restaurant "down under" a bridge which spans the Intracoastal Waterway in Fort Lauderdale. The Down Under is lively, spirited, and the first of a trio of restaurants by the team of Leonce Picot and Al Kocab. Like its sisters Casa Vecchia in Fort Lauderdale and La Vieille Maison in Boca Raton, it's the ultimate in vibrant tasteful decor and freshly delicious cuisine.

Bentwood chairs, wooden floors, plants, warmly inviting brick fireplaces, stained and etched glass, wrought iron balustrades and an al fresco waterfront patio suggest an upbeat, progressive gathering place with a St. Louis-New Orleans jazzy flavor. It's where Fort Lauderdale's young and "young in spirit" gather to unwind, perhaps over a bottle of *Puligny Montrachet* or a splendid California wine. Diners can feel at ease while celebrating that recent promotion with a 1973 *Dom Perignon*, or lingering over Irish Coffee for two while watching boats cruise the Intracoastal.

A multitudinous selection of entrées and appetizers awaits. Chef Christian Planchon has been given free reign in the Down Under's kitchen and has emerged with an exceptional *New Orleans Seafood Gumbo, Oysters Muscovite,* and eleven other cold seafood appetizers, three hot seafood appetizers, and twenty-two seafood entrées—all that plus *Chicken Madagascar, Canard A L'Orange, Veal Napolitaine, Esquire's Carpetbag Steak, Venison Grand Veneur,* and the list seems endless.

The Down Under is a potpourri of memorable sights, sounds, and tastes. It's been an award winner of Florida Trend's Golden Spoon for several years as well as the Travel/ Holiday Magazine Award and Restaurant and Institution Magazine's "Ivy Award."

A sign near the bar on the Down Under's main floor best sums up this restaurant in one word: "Panache!"

When you have found I-95 in Fort Lauderdale, take the Oakland Park Boulevard east exit. Travel east until just before the bridge over the Intracoastal, then exit for address 3000. It's on the right just beside and slightly below the bridge.

Reservations Suggested.

CRIPPEN SALAD

— SALAD —
1-2 large bunches watercress (cleaned and stemmed)
1 can hearts of palm (sliced)
1 cup mushrooms (thinly sliced)
½ cup almonds (sliced and toasted)

— VINAIGRETTE DRESSING —
4 T. olive oil
1 T. vinegar
½ t. salt
½ t. dry mustard
fresh ground pepper

1. Combine all dressing ingredients and shake vigorously.
2. Just before serving, toss all salad ingredients and place on chilled plates.

Serves: 4
Preparation: 15 minutes

"Crisp, light and exotic! !"

MUSHROOMS A LA CREME GEORGE

½ lb. small fresh mushrooms and stems
1 T. butter
1 T. dry sherry
½ cup sour cream (room temperature)
¼ t. M.S.G.
1 t. Worcestershire sauce
1 dash Tabasco
2 slices bread (cut into toast points)
¼ cup butter (melted)
1 T. fresh parsley (chopped)
paprika

1. Sauté mushrooms in butter for 2 minutes.
2. Add sherry. Cook 2 minutes.
3. Add sour cream, M.S.G., Worcestershire and Tabasco. (Consistency should be that of rich hollandaise.)
4. Toast points should be golden and CRISP. Saturate with melted butter.
5. Pour mushrooms on toast points. Sprinkle parsley and paprika over top.

Serves: 1-2 as an appetizer or luncheon course.
Preparation: 10 minutes
Cooking: 6 minutes

"Perfect blend of ingredients for mushrooms. Don't stint on melted butter over the crispy toast points!"

— NOTES —

BRUTUS SALAD

1	clove garlic
1	egg yolk
	juice of 2½ lemons
½	t. ground white pepper
1	cup olive oil
¼	cup green onions (chopped)
¼	t. fresh mint (chopped)
¼	t. oregano
½	cup freshly grated Parmesan or Romano cheese
4	heads Bibb lettuce (well washed)
½	cup bacon (cooked and crumbled)
1	cup croutons
12	cherry tomatoes

1. Sprinkle salt in a large wooden salad bowl. Rub bowl with garlic. Discard garlic.
2. In the bowl, vigorously whip the egg yolk, lemon juice, and white pepper (salt, if necessary). Slowly add olive oil.
3. Mix in green onions, mint, oregano and ¼ of the cheese.
4. Add lettuce and toss. Portion onto chilled plates. Sprinkle with bacon, croutons and remaining cheese. Garnish with tomatoes.

Serves: 4
Preparation: 20 minutes

"A refreshing change from Caesar!"

— NOTES —

RED SNAPPER LOUISIANE

2-3	lbs. red snapper fillets in 4 portions
1	egg
1	cup milk
6	T. butter
	salt and pepper to taste
½	cup flour for dipping
2	cups cooking oil
8	artichoke hearts
4	large fresh mushrooms (sliced)
1	t. Worcestershire sauce
1	t. lemon juice
1	t. tarragon vinegar
½	cup sliced almonds

1. Beat together egg, milk and 2T. melted butter. Salt and pepper to taste.
2. Dip fillets into batter, then in flour. Sauté in oil (as needed) until lightly browned and just done. Keep warm.
3. In another pan, saute artichokes and mushrooms in 2T. butter. Add worcestershire, lemon juice, vinegar. Cook until tender.
4. Toast almonds in 2T. butter under broiler.
5. Place fillets on serving platter. Top with artichokes and mushrooms. Sprinkle with toasted almonds.

Serves: 4
Preparation: 10 minutes
Cooking: 20 minutes

"Ingredients compliment this fine fish!"

— NOTES —

Southeast Tower at Vizcaya, Miami

EL BODEGON CASTILLA
RESTAURANTE ESPAÑOL

miami

El Bodegon Castilla, also known simply as "Castilla", is on the bustling Calle Ocho in Miami. It's a favorite of Miami's Latin community, as well as out-of-towners and no wonder! A delightfully cheerful place, full of aromatic fragrances, it buzzes with conversation in Spanish and English.

Furnishings suggest a Spanish country inn with wooden and leather chairs, open beam ceilings and white stucco walls. Vibrant hand painted murals depict the land of Don Quixote with its mountains, castles, and windmills. A pleasing and simple style so as not to interfere with the excitement of the zesty specialties.

Your polite waiter might suggest beginning the meal with one of the Castilla's hearty and flavorful soups. *Sopa Purrusalda* is a hearty peasant style soup of garlic, potatoes, onions, and chicken. Very fresh and delicious, its flavor suggests the sundrenched Spanish countryside. *Cazuela de Mariscos en Salsa Verde* is a luscious seafood soup-casserole in a "green sauce". Scallops, shrimp, clams, asparagus and parsley are just a few ingredients in this colorful dish. *Medallones "Bodegon"* (Medallions of Tenderloin in a Wine Sauce) or *Filete Madrileña* (Fillet stuffed with Ham and Cheese) are sure to surprise those whose only experience with Spanish cuisine consists of *Paella* or *Arroz con Pollo.* Add a pitcher of *Sangria* or an expresso to complete a mini-trip to Spain.

Jaime Bajo and his partners are ever present at El Bodegon, greeting guests and making certain everything is running smoothly. Their care is evident and their attention to detail is admirable. Among the myriad of Miami's Spanish restaurants, it is certainly "El Primero".

To find E. Bodegon Castilla, take the Palmetto Expressway to U.S. 41 (S.W. 8th St.), then go east on S.W. 8th Street until 27th Avenue. Turn south onto 27th Avenue for one block, then east onto southwest location at 2499 S.W. 8th Street at the corner of 25th Avenue and 8th Street. Parking is behind the restaurant.

Reservations Suggested.

PIPIRRANA DE ALMERIA
(Cod Fish Salad)

½	lb. dry roasted cod fish flakes*
12	stuffed olives (chopped)
1	cucumber (chopped)
1	tomato (peeled & chopped)
1	onion (chopped)
2	cloves garlic (minced)
1	green pepper (chopped)
	black pepper to taste
2	t. olive oil
2	t. red wine vinegar

— GARNISH —
lettuce leaves
hard boiled egg, (chopped)
parsley (chopped)

1. If using cod fish, roast in oven until dry.
2. Mix with remaining ingredients. Add small amount of water.
3. Serve very cold on lettuce leaves. Garnish with egg and parsley.

*NOTE: If not available, substitute fish of your choice. Tuna was delicious! Since Codfish is salty, no salt is needed. When using other fish choice, add salt to taste.

Serves: 6
Preparation: 15 minutes
Chill Well
— NOTES —

MERO EN SALSA VERDE
(Grouper in Green Sauce)

1½	lbs. grouper fillets
1	t. garlic (chopped)
1	t. onion (chopped)
1	t. parsley (chopped)
2	T. oil
2	t. flour
2	cups fish stock
2	T. white wine
8	shrimps
4	clams
4	small potatoes (peeled and boiled)
4-8	asparagus spears
	salt and pepper to taste

1. Sauté garlic, onion and parsley in small amount of oil for 5 minutes. Add flour and blend well.
2. Add stock and wine. Bring to boil and stir.
3. Add remaining ingredients. Bake at 400° for 25 minutes.

Serves: 4
Preparation: 15 minutes
Cooking: 25 minutes

"A meal in one dish, resembling a good fish stew!"

— NOTES —

CORDERO de VALLADOLIO
(Lamb Stew)

2½	lbs. lamb (cubed)
2-3	T. oil
¼	cup onions (diced)
¼	cup celery (diced)
¼	cup carrots (diced)
1	8 oz. can stewed tomatoes
1	bay leaf
½	cup white wine
½	cup brown sauce* (Or use ready made brown gravy in the can.)
	salt and pepper to taste

1. In a large pot, heat oil. Add all ingredients except tomatoes, wine and brown sauce. Stir and cook for 10 minutes.

2. Add tomatoes, wine and brown sauce. Simmer until tender or about 1½ hours.

*See Glossary
Serves: 4
Preparation: 10 minutes
Cook: 10 minutes/1½ hours

"Lamb with a hearty provincial flavor!"
— NOTES —

LECHÉ FRITA
(Fried Milk - Allow time to chill)

1	pt. milk
4	T. cornstarch (mixed with a little of milk)
½	cup plus 2T. sugar
½	t. vanilla
½	cup flour
1	egg (beaten)
½	stick butter (2 oz.)

1. Heat first four ingredients to boiling point, stirring constantly until thickened.
2. Pour in rectangle glass pan. Chill to almost freezing and well set.
3. Cut in small squares. Sprinkle with flour, dip in egg and fry in butter.
4. Serve warm with your favorite chocolate or butterscotch sauce, or perhaps fruit preserves.

Serves: 6
Preparation: 5 minutes
Cooking: 10/10
Chill: 2-3 hours

"Even the name is fun! !"

— NOTES —

miami

One does not merely dine at The Forge. One partakes of a sumptuous experience reminiscent of another era when dining was an art. The Forge Restaurant on Miami Beach not only has won every conceivable dining award, but also was named one of the "50 Best Restaurants" in the United States and was featured at the "A Taste Of America" exhibit during the Presidential Inaugural in 1981. A frequent haunt of socialites since 1930, The Forge was once the site of a real forge, where the famous Dino Phillips created decorative wrought iron gates and other ornamentation for wealthy estates.

Now, chefs create the ultimate in classic cuisine which is a perfect selection of the best in American, Continental, and Nouvelle Cuisine. Rejoice in an appetizer such as *Artichoke Hearts Monte Carlo* with its crabmeat stuffing and memorable sauce. Linger over *Shrimp de Jonge* and savor every plump morsel in a piquant sauce. The *Filet Marie Louise* marinated in cognac and served with truffled pâté de foie gras is an indescribable experience. The ultra rich *Blacksmith Pie* or *Pears in Champagne* are two very elegant desserts that are a perfect culmination to your dining adventure.

Your eyes will be dazzled and delighted with the unforgettable Art Nouveau decor. The tone is plush and opulent — not overstated or extreme. Antique Tiffany lamps and stained glass panels, fragile antique Viennese crystal chandeliers and dore bronze from the Madison era in the White House combine with Napoleonic treasures and old brass ship railings in a luxuriously satisfying manner. The Forge's multi-million dollar wine cellar includes a Chateau Lafite Rothschild 1822 carefully secluded within rows of other wines behind the dazzling 400-pound bronze bank vault door, and a wine book the size of *War and Peace.* In this era of mediocrity and imitation, how refreshing to discover The Forge. All this — and heaven too!

The Forge is located on Miami Beach at 432 Arthur Godfrey Road. Take I-95 to I-195 (Julia Tuttle Causeway) and go east over the causeway. The road will branch into Arthur Godfrey Road (left) and Alton Road (right). Keep to the left and The Forge is on your right after several traffic lights.

Reservations Necessary.

SHRIMP de JONGE

— SHRIMP —

30-36 jumbo shrimp (shelled, deveined and butterflied)

½	cup butter (melted)
3	T. flour
4	shallots (minced)
½	cup dry sherry
2/3	cup heavy cream
	salt and pepper to taste
6	t. parsley (chopped)

— BUTTER CRUMB TOPPING —

1	lb. butter (softened only)
½	t. white pepper
6	shallots (minced)
5	cloves garlic (minced)
10	drops Worcestershire
1	T. dry mustard
2	cups fresh white bread crumbs
	salt to taste

— BUTTER CRUMB TOPPING —

1. Place all topping ingredients in blender or food processor. Blend until smooth. Divide into 6 parts. Set aside.

— SHRIMP —

2. Sauté shrimp in butter 1 minute. Sprinkle with flour and toss. Add shallots and toss to coat shrimp well. Cook 1 minute.
3. Add sherry and cream. Cook and stir about 4-5 minutes until shrimp are just done. (At this point, shrimp may be cooled and refrigerated until ready to use.)
4. When ready to serve, place 5-6 shrimp into 6 oven-proof dishes, pouring sauce over shrimp. Cover with divided topping. Heat in 450° oven 7 minutes, then broil just to brown the topping. Sprinkle with parsley.

-continued-

Serves: 6
Preparation: 15 minutes
Cooking: 12 minutes

"A great method of preparing this famous dish! ! (You just might want to eat all 6 servings yourself!)"

— NOTES —

SNAPPER SINGAPORE

— FILLETS —

6	8 oz. red snapper fillets
	salt and pepper to taste
4	T. clarified butter*
¼	t. thyme
¼	t. tarragon
½	cup dry white wine

— VEGETABLES —

1/3	cup clarified butter
2	green peppers (julienne cut)*
3	red peppers or 3 pimientos (julienne)
1	mild onion (julienne)
½	lb. mushrooms (thinly sliced)
¼	t. tarragon
¼	cup dry sherry
1	T. soy sauce
	salt to taste
	cayenne pepper to taste

— FILLETS —

1. Sprinkle fillets with salt and pepper. Sauté fillets in butter on both sides until tender. Sprinkle with thyme and tarragon and remove to a heated platter.
2. Pour wine into skillet. Reduce* to ½ cup.

— VEGETABLES —

3. In same skillet, heat butter for vegetables. Add peppers and onions. Sauté 2-3 minutes. Should be crisp. Add mushrooms and tarragon. Toss well.
4. Add sherry, soy, salt, cayenne and cook for 2 minutes. Serve over fillets.

*See Glossary
Serves: 6
Preparation: 15 minutes
Cooking: 15-20 minutes

"Crispy colorful vegetables compliment the red snapper."

FILET MARIE LOUISE

— FILETS —
6 filets mignon
½ cup brandy
¼ t. thyme
¼ t. nutmeg
¼ t. black pepper
¼ t. basil
salt to taste
4 T. clarified butter* (to cook filets)

— PÂTÉ de foie GRAS —
1 cup Pâté de foie Gras
(may be purchased in Gourmet Specialty Shops)
¼ cup scallions (minced)
¼ cup heavy cream
3 T. brandy
1-2 T. truffles (minced)
(may be purchased in Gourmet Specialty Shops)
OR use 2-3 T. mushrooms (minced and sautéed)
salt and pepper to taste

— SAUCE —
¼ cup dry sherry
4 T. clarified* butter
6 shallots (minced)
1 cup red wine
2 cloves garlic (minced)
¼ t. thyme
¼ t. chervil
salt and pepper to taste
¼ cup brandy
3 T. truffles (minced)

*See Glossary

-continued-

— PÂTÉ de foie GRAS —

1. Mix all paté ingredients into a smooth paste. Set aside.

— FILETS —

2. Sprinkle filets on all sides with brandy and seasonings. Cover and refrigerate until ready to cook. 30 minutes.

3. In a large skillet, melt clarified butter. Cook filets until browned and done to desired taste. Remove and keep warm.

— SAUCE —

4. De-glaze the skillet with sherry, scraping the sides. Bring to boil and pour into a sauce pan.

5. Add butter and shallots. Cook until transparent (about 6 minutes). Add wine, garlic, thyme, chervil and salt and pepper to taste. Cook and reduce* by ¼.

6. Add brandy and truffles and cook until slightly thick (if using truffles, add at the last just to heat). To serve, top each filet with 2-3 T. sauce and, using a pastry bag, pipe a rosette of pâté de foie gras on each filet.

*See Glossary
Serves: 6
Preparation: 20 minutes
Cooking: 8-10 minutes

"This is divine! !"

— NOTES —

Joe's
STONE CRAB RESTAURANT

miami

One of the true Florida legends in its own time is Joe's Stone Crab Restaurant. Located at the absolute tip of Miami Beach, it was founded by Joe Weiss, a waiter who came to Miami from New York in 1913. In those days, most of Miami Beach was visited only by pelicans. Joe's Restaurant, as it was called, was originally a frame house where Joe and his wife toiled over smoky kerosene stoves to serve their guests tasty "shore dinners." Later, in 1923, Joe "discovered" that tender delicacy, the Stone Crab, and added them to the menu. The immediate popularity of the new house specialty led to a new christening of the present stucco building . . .Joe's Stone Crab.

Today, another "Joe" is in charge of Joe's Stone Crab Restaurant. Joe Weiss's granddaughter, Jo-Ann, and her husband, Irwin Sawitz, continue the family traditions passed from Joe to his son Jesse.

The overwhelming demand for Stone Crabs caused quite a shortage through the years, so now only legal sized claws are taken instead of the entire crab. They are prepared and served chilled with melted butter. Add homestyle cole slaw and luscious cottage fries, and you have ecstacy "a la Florida". An impressive list of Florida seafood from *Yellowtail* and *Pompano*, to *Shrimp* and *Oysters* entice hungry diners at Joe's.

The decor is rustic - a fish house style of stark simplicity with white stucco walls, a handpainted ceiling, tile and terazzo floors. Photos on the walls depict early Florida, a real education to the many of us who have only recently arrived from the North. It's a restaurant that proves frills and fancy decor are not necessary to have an award winning establishment. Joe's Stone Crab has won the Travel/Holiday Magazine award yearly since 1961.

Joe's Stone Crab Restaurant is more than a legend, or an institution — is IS Florida ! !

Joe's Stone Crab Restaurant is located at the very end of Miami Beach at 227 Biscayne Street. Take I-95 to A1A (U.S. 41), which runs into the Douglas MacArthur Causeway. Go east over the causeway to Alton Road, then south on Alton Road to Biscayne Street.

No Reservations Accepted.

SEVICHE
(Allow 4 hours or more to Marinate)

1	lb. bay scallops (or sea scallops cut smaller)
6	scallions (white part only-chopped)
1	cup lime juice
½	cup orange juice
6	T. onion (chopped fine)
4	T. parsley (chopped fine)
2	T. green pepper (chopped fine)
½	cup olive oil
½	t. oregano
1	t. salt
	ground pepper
	crushed red pepper to taste
	Tabasco to taste

1. Marinate scallops and scallions in lime juice and orange juice (at least 4 hours.) Drain well and discard marinade.
2. Add remaining ingredients, mix and serve on lettuce leaves.

Serves: 6 as an appetizer
Preparation: 10 minutes
Chill: 4 hours

"This goes over very well with guests! !"
— NOTES —

La Reserve

The Norman Conquest, contrary to popular opinion, did not occur in England in 1066, but when Guy and Richard Teboul brought La Reserve to Fort Lauderdale. Along with their brother Leon, who owns Le Cafe' Du Beaujolais, Guy and Richard have created waves of applause from Florida's East coast residents and visitors.

The elegant cuisine is truly French, from the *Cuisses De Grenouille Provencale*, (Frog Legs Sautéed in Garlic Butter) to the creamy *Camembert*. Veal predominated the menu with three different style cutlets, *Escalope De Veau Au Smyrne*, with its raisins and Port Sauce, the *Forestiere* with Sherry and Mushroom Sauce and the extra succulent *De Veau Poilee au Citron* with its butter and lemon sauce. Accent your veal selection with an offering of *Bisque De Homard*, the lovely lobster bisque or the *Langouste Mayonnaise*, a half Florida lobster served with the Chef's special mayonnaise.

Other pleasing seafood *entrées* include the *Snapper Deauville*, poached fillet of Red Snapper and the *Langouste Aux Courgettes*, fresh Florida lobster in light wine sauce and zucchini.

For dessert, the spectacular pastry cart is filled with irresistable delights such as *Almond Cake* and *Finnish pastry*.

The charming Richard and Guy Teboul proudly describe the recent awards La Reserve has collected. Among them are the Travel/Holiday Magazine Award and United Mainliner. A former Parisian, Teboul proudly describes the restaurant as "French cuisine with a California accent."

La Reserve is the type of restaurant where you could easily enjoy a soul-satisfying three-hour dinner. With an attentive captain, solicitous service from the attentive waiters, and ever-changing vistas, you are totally removed from everyday matters and obligations. In fact, you were born to be pampered — like all the other kings and queens of the world seated around you.

The architecture is new, modern, and cantilevered with four levels of dining areas allowing every diner a spectacular view of the Intracoastal Waterway. The spacious dining room is alive with laughter, with French and English bantered good naturedly between waiters and patrons. In the corner, a young couple gazes into each other's eyes while toasting the future with *Moet et Chandon*. Simple elegance in shades of dusty rose blend with rough hewn cypress and hanging plants to lend a relaxed elegance! Fresh gladiolas and carnations suggest that extra touch of natural beauty and romance. Romance — isn't that how French Cuisine and dreams were born?

La Reserve is certainly not inexpensive - but then anything precious and rare carries a price. At La Reserve, the price is most certainly an accurate statement of the worth — and you are worth every cent.

To discover La Reserve, take I-95 to the Oakland Park Blvd. East exit. Travel east as far as the Intracoastal exit directly after the bridge for 3115 N.E. 32nd Avenue. La Reserve is on the Intracoastal, beside and just slightly north of the bridge.

Reservations Suggested.

VEGETABLE PÂTÉ
(Allow Time to Chill)

4	eggs
1¼	cups carrots (cooked and finely diced)
1¼	cups spinach (cooked and finely diced)
1¼	cups cauliflower (cooked and finely diced)
1¼	cups green beans (cooked and finely diced)
	salt and pepper to taste
½	cup dressing (Recipe to follow)
1	tomato (for garnish)
	parsley (for garnish)
	lettuce leaves (for garnish)

– DRESSING –

1	egg yolk
1	T. Dijon mustard
	salt and pepper
2	oz. vinegar
8	oz. salad oil
	cayenne to taste

– DRESSING –

1. Whisk by hand, or use a blender of food processor to blend egg yolk and mustard. Add salt and pepper.
2. VERY SLOWLY pour in oil, a drop at a time.
3. Slowly add vinegar and a touch of cayenne. Chill. Yield: 1 cup.

"We found this dressing delightful. However, if you lack the time to prepare it, perhaps you might add a dash of Dijon mustard and a T. of lemon juice to your favorite mayonnaise!"

– PÂTÉ –

4. Mix each vegetable separately with beaten egg, salt and pepper.

-continued-

5. Layer each vegetable in a rectangular baking dish (9" X 12"). Start with carrots and end with green beans on top. Place it in a larger baking dish filled with water.
6. Bake 2½ hours at 275°. Chill several hours or overnight.
7. To serve, cut in slices. Place on flat lettuce leaf. Garnish with tomato wedge, chopped parsley and a dollop of dressing.

Serves: 6-8
Preparation: 30 minutes
Cooking: 2½ hours
Chill: 4 hours

"Beautiful to serve and a very different salad course! !"

— NOTES —

FILLET ST. AMOUR

4	8 oz. fillets
1	red onion (chopped)
4	T. butter
2	cups red wine
½	t. thyme
1	bay leaf
2	cups veal stock (you may use chicken without fat)
	parsley (chopped for garnish)

1. Sauté onion in butter. When cooked, remove ¾ of onion and reserve.
2. To the remaining onion, add wine and seasonings. Simmer and reduce*by ½.
3. Add stock. Taste for seasoning. Keep warm.
4. Cook steaks to desired doneness. Top with reserved onion, then sauce. Garnish with parsley.

*See Glossary
Serves: 4
Preparation: 5 minutes
Cooking: 10/10

— NOTES —

FLORIDA LOBSTER ZUCCHINI

2-3 Florida lobsters (cooked meat removed from tail and sliced)
   OR 1 lb. lobster meat (cooked)
2 zucchini (sliced)
1 tomato (peeled and cubed)

— WINE SAUCE —
4-5 shallots or ½ red onion (chopped)
½ stick butter
1 cup white wine
2 cups fish stock*
3 T. flour
   chopped parsley for garnish
1 cup heavy cream

— WINE SAUCE —
1. Sauté shallots in ½ of the butter (¼ stick). Add wine and reduce* by ¼. Add stock. Simmer 15 minutes.
2. Combine remaining butter and 3T. flour. Cook in a small pan until golden. Slowly add stock to this. Return to stock pan, stirring until blended.
3. Add cream. Stir until slightly thickened. Season to taste.
4. Cook zucchini 2-3 minutes in boiling water. Cool.

— LOBSTER —
5. Add lobster to heat in ¾ of sauce. Put on plate. Top with zucchini. Mix tomato with remaining ¼ sauce. Pour over top. Garnish with parsley.

*See Glossary
Serves: 4
Preparation: 10 minutes
Cooking: 20-25 minutes

"A very attractive dish to serve. And the taste is superb!"

La Vieille Maison

One "old house" which decided to begin an exciting new life as a great restaurant is La Vieille Maison. Since 1976, La Vieille Maison has enchanted residents of Boca Raton and socialite "commuters" of nearby Palm Beach, with its cuisine of Provence and the French and Italian Riviera.

This is the second restaurant in the thrilling Leonce Picot-Al Kocab trilogy of award winners. La Vieille Maison has been garnering the lavish praise of the area restaurant critics as well as Travel/Holiday, Mobil Guide Five Stars, Florida Trend Golden Spoon and United Mainliner. Their Lobster Bisque was featured in the 1981 Taste of America exhibit at the Presidential Inauguration.

An historic old house from the Addison Mizner era, La Vieille Maison whispers an architecturally Mediterranean heritage. (Addison Mizner was the architect responsible for promoting the elegant Spanish-Mediterranean style in Florida.) It's a house full of intimate dining rooms, balconies, antiques, lithographs, hanging plants and fresh flowers, wrought iron gates, festivity and graciousness. The dining rooms are arranged around a refreshing central courtyard, an idea that's typically Spanish.

Dine in luxury on French china with thin stemmed crystal. Nibble on *Faisan Fumé* (smoked pheasant with mustard or cumberland sauce) or try a first course of the *Salad Composée*. It's almost too beautifully arranged to eat! For a second course perhaps the *Crevettes Au Pernod* (jumbo shrimp sautéed with onions, green peppers, tomatoes, garlic and Pernod), a *Pompano "en papillote"*, or *Saddle of Scottish Venison.* Decisions, decisions! And as in his other restaurants, Leonce Picot has assembled an exceptionally fine wine list, heavily favoring the excellent California wines.

Memorable cuisine, service and decor. . .a dining event to be cherished. . .La Vieille Maison.

To find La Vieille Maison in Boca Raton, go east from I-95 at the Palmetto Park Road exit. It's at 770 E. Palmetto Park Road, just on the right after the Intracoastal Waterway.

Reservations Suggested.

FLORIDA LOBSTER BISQUE

2	2 lb. lobsters
1	carrot (finely chopped)
1	onion (finely chopped)
1	stalk celery (finely chopped)
½	lb. butter
2	cups white wine
2	quarts fish stock*
½	t. thyme
3	bay leaves
½	cup rice
12	peppercorns
1	cup tomato puree
2	cups heavy cream
1	cup brandy
	salt and pepper to taste

1. Separate lobster heads from tails. Cook tails in water 10 minutes. Set aside.
2. Sauté lobster heads, carrot, onion and celery in ¼ lb. butter, until lightly colored.
3. Add wine, stock, thyme, bay leaves, rice, peppercorns, tomato purée and salt to taste. Simmer 45 minutes.
4. Strain bisque through fine sieve. Bring to second boil. Check seasoning. Add remaining ¼ lb. butter. Add cream and brandy.
5. Dice meat from lobster tails. Add to bisque and serve.

*See Glossary
Serves: 12
Preparation: 15 minutes
Cooking: 10/50 minutes

"Very Rich. . .small servings enhance this very fine soup!"

CAILLE AUX RAISINS
(Quail with Grapes)

4	4 oz. quails
4	thin slices bacon
3	doz. white seedless grapes
1½	oz. cognac
5	oz. demi-glace*

1. Wrap each quail in bacon slice. Place in lightly greased sauté pan. Cook covered about 10 minutes, turning. Place uncovered in hot oven 400° for 12-15 minutes or until done.
2. Remove from oven and flambé carefully with brandy. Place on warm platter.
3. Add grapes and demi-glace to sauté pan drippings. Blend well.
4. Pour sauce over birds and let it spread elegantly on the bottom of platter.

*See Glossary
Serves: 2
Preparation: 10 minutes
Cooking: 30 minutes

"These delectable little birds done a La Vieille Maison always bring raves! !"

— NOTES —

Le Café Du Beaujolais

Like his brothers Richard and Guy, Leon Teboul also owns a French restaurant in Fort Lauderdale. Fine cuisine runs in the family. Leon's is Le Café du Beaujolais, the more "French" in decor of the two. Delicate gauze Viennese style curtains grace the windows. Bright red chairs contrast with crisp, white table linens, and greenery abounds in white brick room dividers. The red striped wallpaper is a very striking visual effect in the main dining room, in much the same manner as the polished brass espresso machine in the lounge.

Leon, a former chef, and his wife Giselle are busily involved in the day to day operation of Le Café du Beaujolais. It may be that while Leon is the "heart" of Le Café du Beaujolais, Giselle is its "soul". Her little decorative touches enliven the room and her lighthearted spirit pervades.

It's all very French from the decor to the *Quiche Lorraine* and *Escargots de Bourgogne*. The very popular *Soupe* à l' *Oignon Gratin*ée is a favorite! The *Lapin Sauce Moutarde*, rabbit in a mustard sauce, and *Ris De Veau* à *La Creme,* veal sweetbreads braised in a white cream sauce are slightly different specialties that enliven the diner who is bored by the beef-fish-foul syndrome. There's a well stocked wine cellar for those who wish to partake of the grape.

In the French tradition of appearance being the "calling card" of quality, you will be beckoned to sample the beautiful, and no doubt rich, pastries and creamy desserts prepared fresh daily. Le Café du Beaujolais is pretty, Parisian, and as they say in France, "parfait".

The address of Le Cafe Du Beaujolais is 3134 N.E. 9th Street in Fort Lauderdale. Take the Sunrise Blvd. exit off I-95 and go east to the beach where Sunrise Blvd. meets A1A. Go south for a block, then turn west on N.E. 9th Street. Le Cafe Du Beaujolais is on the left.

Reservations Suggested.

FILET DeSOLE DINARD

2   Dover sole fillets
8-10 oz. white wine
      salt and pepper to taste
1   carrot (julienne cut)*
1/3 oz. black truffles**
2   egg yolks
2   oz. heavy cream
1/3 cup melted butter

1. Poach fillets in wine, salt, pepper and enough water to cover, (about 8-10 minutes) or until just done.
2. Remove fish to a warmed oven-proof platter. Add carrots and truffles to sauce. Cook and reduce.

3. Mix egg yolks and cream. Whisk into sauce. Pour over fish. Top with butter and brown under broiler.

  *See Glossary.
**Mushrooms may be substituted here if necessary.
Serves: 2
Preparation: 10 minutes
Cook: 15 minutes

"A delicacy! !"

— NOTES —

LAPIN WITH SAUCE MOUTARDE
(Rabbit in a Mustard Sauce)

1	rabbit (cut in pieces) about 2 lbs.
2	T. butter
4	shallots (chopped)
½	t. thyme
1	bay leaf
1	cup white wine
1	T. Pommery mustard (may be purchased at Gourmet Specialty Shops or substitute french mustard with champagne)
3	cups veal stock*

1. Sauté rabbit in butter until golden brown, 15 minutes.
2. Add shallots and sauté 1 minute more.
3. Mix mustard, wine, stock and seasonings together. Pour over rabbit, cover and simmer 1 - 1¼ hours. Serve with rice.

*See Glossary

Serves: 4
Preparation: 10 minutes
Cooking: 1½hours

"We liked this with mildly seasoned wild rice!"

— NOTES —

✚ LES TROIS MOUSQUETAIRES

It's "all for one and one for all" at this Fort Lauderdale restaurant. Les Trois Mousquetaires is the creation of Andre Labouri and his partners. It features the traditional best in French cuisine, in an intimate atmosphere. Gold and cream-color brocade wallpaper above dark brown wainscoting, brown provincial chairs, banquettes and potted plants, suggest a tiny French parlour. Mousquetaire accoutrements, capes and swords are displayed as wall decorations, as well as framed awards, and other plaques the restaurant has received. One of the most recent is the Travel/Holiday Magazine Award.

From the escargot and the *Vichyssoise*, to the pastry cart, it's oh so French! The Delicate *Mousse de Saumon* is one of Les Trois Mousquetaires most favorite appetizers. Andre often recommends the *Moules Marinieres*. They're mussels steamed in white wine and served with shallots, herbs and parsley, and very fresh and tender. Veal and its myriad of sauces are in abundance but the sauces are light and delicate, so as not to fatigue the palate. *Poulet des Mousquetaires* is the restaurant's savory chicken dish served with artichoke hearts, mushrooms and sautéed potatoes. *Squab in Casserole* is an entrée not usually found on most French menus. It's a dish to be savored with your favorite French wine.

The perfect ending to a lunch or dinner at Les Trois Mousquetaires is a heavenly *Chocolate Mousse* or one of the delicate Napoleons. (Are we quite certain he *lost* at Waterloo?) It's a definite victory when one surrenders to French cuisine.

Les Trois Mousquetaires, we salute you!

From I-95 in Fort Lauderdale, take the Sunrise Blvd. East exit to 2447. Les Trois Mousquetaires is in the International Building.

Reservations Suggested.

MOULES MARINIERES
(Mussles in Wine Sauce)

4	lbs. fresh mussels (well washed and scrubbed to remove all sand)
1	cup water
1	cup wine
½	stick butter (2 oz.)
1	onion (chopped)
4	cloves garlic (minced)
2	T. fresh parsley (chopped)
1	stalk celery (chopped)
3	T. flour
2	cups white wine (strain through fine napkin)
1	cup fish stock*
	salt and coarse black pepper to taste
¼	t. curry powder
1½	t. basil
1½	t. tarragon
1½	t. thyme
1½	t. oregano

1. Steam mussels in water and 1 cup wine for about 8 minutes or until opened. Rinse very well to ensure sand is gone. Remove mussels from shell. Reserve both mussels and shells.
2. Melt butter and sauté onions, garlic, parsley and celery. Add mussels and cook 2 minutes. Stir in flour. Cook 1 minute.
3. Add wine and stock, seasonings and herbs. Simmer 4 minutes.
4. Place mussels in shells. Spoon sauce over all.

*See Glossary
Serves: 8
Preparation: 30 minutes
Cooking: 8/10

"Enjoy with a light California wine and crusty French bread."

L'ESCALOPE NORMANDE
(Scallops of Tender Veal)

6	5 oz. escalopes of veal (scalloppine pounded flat to ¼")
	salt and pepper to taste
	flour for dredging
3	oz. butter
3	oz. oil
6	oz. mushrooms (sliced)
2	T. Calvados
1	cup chablis
1	pint heavy cream

1. Salt and pepper and lightly dredge the veal. Sauté in butter and oil. Put on serving platter and keep warm.
2. Sauté mushrooms in drippings, add Calvados and chablis. Reduce* about 5 minutes or until almost gone. gone.
3. Add cream and reduce until thick. Pour over veal and serve.

*See Glossary
Serves: 6
Preparation: 15 minutes
Cooking: 15 minutes

"A creamy brandy flavor! !"

— NOTES —

POULET DES MOUSQUETAIRES
(Roast Chicken with Herbs)

1	roasting chicken (cleaned)
2	t. basil
2	t. thyme
2	t. oregano
	salt and pepper to taste

— SAUCE —

1	cup white wine
1	cup veal stock*

— GARNITURE —

12-16	tiny potatoes (peeled, cut to large olive size)
3	oz. oil
20	mushrooms (cut in half)
2	shallots (chopped)
1	whole artichoke heart (cooked and quartered)
1	small clove garlic (minced)
½	cup parsley (chopped)
	pinch of basil
	salt and pepper to taste
1	oz. butter

1. Mix basil, thyme, oregano, salt and pepper. Sprinkle inside chicken. Roast ten minutes at 400º. Then, 30 minutes at 350º or until juices run clear.

— GARNITURE —

2. Saute' potatoes in oil 6 minutes until tender. Add mushrooms, saute' 1 minute. Add shallots, artichoke heart, garlic, parsley, basil, salt and pepper. Heat. Drain off oil. Replace with 1 oz. butter.

*See Glossary

-continued-

— SAUCE —

3. When chicken is cooked, remove to warm serving platter.

4. Brown juices 1 minute on stove. Spoon off grease. Add wine and stock. Boil and reduce* 5 minutes.

5. To serve, place garniture around chicken. Pour sauce over chicken and vegetables.

*See Glossary
Serves: 4
Preparation: 15 minutes
Cooking: 45-50 minutes

"Succulent chicken, tasting of herbs. Attractive Garnish!"

— NOTES —

Marker 88

plantation key

Ah. . .the Florida Keys! Still a refuge of natural beauty created by the crystal clear joining of the Gulf and the Atlantic, miles of undeveloped beach line, unique and colorful sealife, and equally as unique and colorful, residents, are part of the ever changing vista.

About one-third of the way through the Keys is Marker 88 Restaurant, so named because it is located beside mile marker 88 on the highway. Its owner, Andre Mueller is a hardy "vagabond chef". Having begun his culinary career in Switzerland as apprentice to some of Europe's great chefs, he then travelled to Bermuda, Hawaii, New York and finally ended his wanderlust in the Florida Keys, where the slower pace of life suits him.

The cuisine of Marker 88 reflects Andre's globe-trotting career with exotic entrees such as *Steak Madagascar*, appetizers such as *Oysters Moscow* and *Cajun Seafood Gumbo*. The native specialty of the Keys, the conch, is frequently listed on the menu. For those unfamiliar with this delicacy, the conch is a mollusk that lives in a gorgeous pink lipped shell — a nautical poor man's escargot with the texture of clams, and a rich flavor all its own. You must try the *Conch Chowder*, a Keys tradition! Top the meal off with a slice of *Key Lime Pie "a la Andre"*.

Andre's chosen decor for Marker 88 is a "seashore eclectic". Chunks of driftwood, pecky cypress paneling, seashells and open beam ceilings mix with tiffany style lamps and hanging plants. Large picture windows enable diners to view the spectacular waterfront. It's a view that goes on for miles, and for years in your memory. The restaurant has a comfortable, homey atmosphere much like the Keys in its island informality. It has been critically acclaimed as the "Best Restaurant" in the Keys. In the semi-uncharted, sprawling wilderness, how refreshing to see this little beacon of gourmandaise!

The Florida Keys are easy to find — just keep going south on the Florida Turnpike until it's impossible to go any further. Pick up Route 1. Stay on Route 1 to mile marker 88, and you've found Marker 88 Restaurant!

Reservations Suggested.

CONCH BISQUE

8-12 oz. conch meat (cleaned, peeled and ground. See Note*)
2   quarts cold water
     bouquet garni (See Note** Make this first)
2   T. salt
4   T. flour
2   T. butter
½   cup heavy cream
     sherry

1. Place the conch, cold water, bouquet garni and salt in large pan and bring to a boil. Simmer 1½ hours.
2. Discard bouquet garni. Strain soup and put meat aside, reserving broth.
3. In a sauce pan, make a *roux (*See Glossary) with butter and flour. Add strained soup, stirring constantly until thickened slightly. Add conch.
4. Return to boil and simmer 15 minutes more. Add cream and heat. Serve with sherry on the side, to be added according to taste.

Serves: 4
Preparation: 10 minutes
Cooking: 1¾ hours

*NOTE: Chopped clams or any edible whelk may be substituted.
**NOTE: BOUQUET GARNI:
    2 sprigs fresh parsley
    1 stalk celery
    1 leek
    1 large piece fresh ginger halved, tied together with string.

"There are many ways to prepare conch in a soup. This bisque is rich and creamy!"

LOBSTER MEXICALI

— CHEESE SAUCE —

6	oz. sharp cheddar cheese
2	cups milk
4	T. flour
2	T. butter
	dash of nutmeg

— LOBSTER —

4	1 lb. Florida lobsters or 1 lb. lobster meat.*
	juice of 1 lemon
2	T. Worcestershire sauce
	salt to taste
4	T. olive oil
1	onion (diced)
2	green peppers (diced)
1	small jar pimientos (diced)
½	cup Parmesan grated
½	cup Swiss (grated)
½	cup mozzarella (grated)

— CHEESE SAUCE —

1. In a sauce pan, heat cheese and milk until blended.
2. Make a roux (See Glossary) of the flour and butter. Add to cheese mixture, stirring constantly until thickened. Stir in nutmeg. (Yield: About 2½ cups; may be made in advance and even frozen.)

*NOTE: If using just lobster meat, distribute among ramekins or scallop shells and proceed as in step 3.

— LOBSTER —

3. Trim lobsters of antennae and legs. Clean chest cavities. Remove meat from tails, leaving shells intact.
4. Season tail meat with lemon ·juice, Worcestershire and salt. Sauté in oil with onion, green pepper and pimiento. Simmer 5 minutes.

-continued-

— TO ASSEMBLE —

5. Distribute meat mixture among shells. Top each with some cheese sauce and a little of each grated cheese. Place under broiler until cheese is melted and browned.

Serves: 4
Preparation: 25 minutes
Cooking: 15 minutes

"Do yourself a favor by sampling this unusual dish! !"

— NOTES —

KEY LIME BAKED ALASKA
(Allow 24 hours to Freeze)

---

4   **eggs (separated)**
1   **can sweetened condensed milk**
½   **cup key lime juice**
½   **gallon brick vanilla ice cream**
½   **t. cream of tartar**
½   **cup sugar**
      grated chocolate or toasted almonds

1. Beat egg yolks. Blend in sweetened condensed milk. Add lime juice.
2. Cut ice cream into 1" slices. Arrange one-half of the slices on bottom of loaf pan. Pour egg mixture over this. Top with layer of remaining ice cream. Freeze overnight.
3. Unmold on brown paper and replace in freezer for 15 minutes*

— FROSTING —
4. Beat egg whites with cream of tartar, until very stiff. Gradually add sugar and beat. Frost ice cream mold with the meringue (about ½" thick.) Sprinkle with chocolate or almonds.
5. Place on a bread board (the reason for this - so heat won't melt ice cream on bottom of mold.) Bake in 500° oven 5 minutes, watching carefully.

*NOTE: Before frosting, the mold may be kept in the freezer indefinitely, allowing you to use just the amount needed and save the rest for another time. After frosting, it will keep in the freezer nicely for 2 days before baking.

Serves: 12
Preparation: 10/10 minutes
Chill: 24 hours
Bake: 5 minutes

"Our lovely Florida Key Limes make this a tropical delight!"

Petite

Marmite

Worth Avenue
Palm Beach

The Petite Marmite, whose name in French means "the little earthen cooking pot" is a restaurant in Palm Beach that has been delighting the socialites of that area for decades. It has a truly cosmopolitan atmosphere — panel paintings of Capri by Luigi de Gregorio and murals by Florentine still life painter Riccardo Magni recall the sunny spirit of the Old World. Wrought iron grillwork gates welcome patrons at the entrance. A vibrant courtyard of plants, red awnings and rich clay tile floors lead to a cheerful skylight room with a gracefully arched brick wall of soothing earth tones. Hanging ferns are everywhere, fresh carnations grace each table, tablecloths are a garden motif-pink and rose flowers and green leaves peek out behind a white trellis on each cloth. Green carpeting and chair seats of rose red or bright green further enhance the charming garden mood.

The Petite Marmite is the spirit of Palm Beach with a slightly Mediterranean "joie de vivre" that reflects the homeland of owner Constanzo "Gus" Pucillo. Born in Capri, he traveled to Rome, Switzerland, and Paris to learn from great chefs of Europe before coming to America after World War II. His restaurant then became, and still is, the rage of Palm Beach society. Visiting dignitaries and celebrities such as Liberace, Gloria Swanson, and Jordan's King Hussein have dined at the Petite.

Perhaps they sampled the *Broiled Shrimp Scampi, Tournedos Henri IV,* or other fine entrées, or concluded their elegant supper with *Parfait à la Menthe* or *Cherries Jubilee.* Whatever they sampled from the Petite Marmite, it was certain to be memorable. This award winning restaurant has been the recipient of the Travel/Holiday Award since 1967, the Florida Trend Golden Spoon Award and the International Copa D'Oro (Gold Cup) Award. The "little cooking pot" will bubble merrily in the hearts and minds of Floridians as well as international visitors for decades yet to come.

The Petite Marmite is located in Palm Beach on fashionable Worth Avenue at number 315. Take I-95 to Southern Blvd. just south of West Palm Beach. Exit and proceed east as far as possible, over the Intracoastal Waterway to South Ocean Blvd. Go north on South Ocean Blvd. past stately mansions to Worth Avenue. Then go west on Worth Avenue (it's a one-way street) to the Petite Marmite, which is on your right.

Reservations Suggested.

MOULES POULETTE
(Mussels in Cream Sauce)

4	lbs. fresh mussels (well cleaned and scrubbed to remove all sand)
2	cups water
2	cups white wine
	juice of 1 lemon
2	shallots (chopped)
¼	lb. butter
1	cup flour
3	egg yolks
½	lb. heavy cream
	salt and pepper to taste
1	bunch parsley (chopped)

1. Place the mussels in a large pot with water, wine and lemon juice. Steam 7-8 minutes or until shells open. (Reserve liquid).
2. Place each mussel on shell half. Arrange on large heat-proof platter (or individual plates).
3. Strain liquid through a cloth napkin.
4. Sauté shallots in butter. Add flour, stirring constantly with a whisk until smooth. Add reserved liquid. Stir until medium thick.
5. Beat in egg yolks, cream and parsley, stirring. Taste for seasoning.
6. Anoint the mussels with sauce and serve hot.

Serves: 4 as entrée, 8 as appetizer
Preparation: 20-30 minutes
Cooking: 8/10 minutes

"The mussel is a fine mollusk, when lovingly handled and sauced. A nice variation if one is bored with clams and scallops. Delectable!"

SHRIMP SCAMPI

—BROILED SHRIMP —

3	lbs. shrimp* (peeled, deveined with tails left on)
½	cup oil
½	cup fresh bread crumbs
	salt and pepper to taste

—SCAMPI SAUCE —

3	shallots (ground or finely minced)
1	clove garlic (ground or finely minced)
2	T. Worcestershire sauce
1	cup lemon juice
1	cup sherry
1	lb. butter (softened)
1½	cup american mustard (yellow)

— SHRIMP –

1. Split shrimp half way to tail. Arrange in oven proof dishes. Brush with oil. Sprinkle with bread crumbs. Put aside.

— SCAMPI SAUCE —

2. Mix shallots, garlic, Worcestershire, lemon juice and sherry in sauce pan.
3. Mix butter and mustard, add to sauce pan. Boil 5 minutes, stirring constantly. (May be stored in refrigerator for weeks, as lemon juice preserves the mixture)

* Petite Marmite uses imported red shrimp from Spain for this recipe.

— SHRIMP SCAMPI —

4. Broil shrimp 5 minutes, being careful not to burn. Pour warmed sauce over shrimp to serve.

-continued-

PETITE MARMITE

Serves: 6-8
Preparation: 25 minutes
Cooking: 5/5minutes

"Mustard makes this scampi preparation a little different and surprisingly exciting. Memorably enhanced with sips of Soave, a strong wine from Italy's Verona region."

— NOTES —

BREAST OF CHICKEN MAISON

6	whole chicken breasts (halved, skinned, boned. Flatten until thin between wax paper.)
10	chicken livers
½	lb. butter
	salt and pepper to taste
1	cup flour
2	eggs (beaten)
3	cups fresh white bread crumbs
½	lb. butter

1. Sauté livers in 2T. butter. Grind or put in food processor.
2. Place about 2T. of ground livers on each of 6 breast halves. Salt and pepper. Top with other half and press together, to form six cutlets of even shape.
3. Dip cutlets in flour, then in beaten egg. Roll them in bread crumbs.
4. Sauté cutlets on one side, in butter until golden. Turn over, sauté other side. Place in hot oven 400º for 10-15 minutes until tender.

Serves: 6
Preparation: 20 minutes
Cooking: 25 minutes

"Liver fanciers will delight in this! ! A chance to enjoy chicken livers in a supremely prepared entrée!"

— NOTES —

THE PLUM ROOM

ft. lauderdale

Upstairs at Yesterday's — one of Fort Lauderdale's lively nightspots, is the elegant, very secluded Plum Room. A sophisticated setting of burgundy and shining crystal awaits those select few who choose to leisurely dine in style.

Admission to the Plum Room is by the use of a gold card inserted into the door. Cards are obtained from the hostess upon arrival for those who have made proper reservations and possibly even "pass inspection". This gives the illusion of a private club and also serves to keep the curious at bay. It's a small, intimate room carefully furnished — a limited number of tables and cushiony velvet banquettes with bolster pillows. The lighting is subdued by the use of spotlights that illuminate only the table, leaving the diners alone in the romantic shadows.

Into this quiet luxury, area gourmets can retreat to sample *Les Medaillions de Veau Casimir* or *Le Pheasant Perigourdine* from a menu that is indeed French influenced. Entrées such as *Venison with Pepper Sauce* and *Elk in Green Pepper Sauce* are available, as well as such unusual delicacies as lion or buffalo. The more exotic meats require advance notice and extra preparation time, as the meticulous chef requires them to be marinated. However, the venison and elk are standard menu items.

In their consummate effort to please, the Plum Room staff will prepare special items at a customer's request. The waiters are competent and caring, not icily haughty nor overly familiar — a credit to owner Peter Goldhahn. His reserved manner and dedication to his art is reflected in every facet of the Plum Room: decor, food and most particularly, the service.

In Fort Lauderdale the Plum Room speaks softly but creates an unforgettable impact on the discerning gourmet.

The Plum Room is upstairs at Yesterday's, 3001 E. Oakland Park Blvd. Take I-95 to the Oakland Park Blvd. east exit and go east almost to the Intracoastal Waterway. Take the avenue exit just before the bridge for number 3001.

Reservations Necessary.

LA CASSOLETTE D'ESCARGOTS VIGNERONNE
(Snails, Mushrooms, and Chablis)

24	escargot
2	T. butter
½	cup mushrooms (quartered)
¼	cup shallots (chopped)
1	oz. brandy
¼	cup chablis (white wine)
¼	cup heavy cream
½	cup Sauce Bordelaise*
¼	cup parsley (chopped)

1. Sauté drained escargots, shallots and mushrooms in butter 3-4 minutes.
2. De-glaze* pan with brandy and white wine.
3. Add cream and Sauce Bordelaise. Reduce.*
4. To serve, place in small bowls and sprinkle with parsley.

*See Glossary
Serves: 3-4
Preparation: 5 minutes
Cook: 10 minutes

"Escargot fanciers will find this fantastic!"

— NOTES —

ALASKAN KING CRAB LEGS DIJONAISE

9-12 3" pieces king crab legs (take from shell)
1   4 oz. jar Dijon mustard (Grey Poupon)
1   cup seasoned bread crumbs
¼   t. garlic powder
¼   lb. butter
1   cup Sauce Beárnaise*
½   cup fresh whipped cream
      chopped parsley
      parsley sprig

1. Dredge crab legs in mustard. Lightly roll in bread crumbs, sprinkled with garlic powder.
2. Sauté in butter until browned. Place in individual baking dishes.
3. Mix Sauce Béarnaise with whipped cream. Nap the crab legs.
4. Place under broiler until golden brown. Garnish with chopped parsley and one sprig of parsley.

*See Glossary
Serves: 3-4
Preparation: 10 minutes
Cooking: 10 minutes

"One of the great delights in fine appetizers! !"

— NOTES —

SNAPPER RIVIERA

4	6 oz. fillets of red snapper
	flour for dusting
½	lb. butter
¾	cup scallions (sliced)
1	cup mushrooms (sliced)
10	oz. Alaskan king crab legs (cut into 1/4" pieces)
1/3	cup chablis
1	cup Sauce Bordelaise*
	juice from 2 lemons
1	cup fresh spinach (shredded)

1. Lightly dust fillets with flour. Sauté in 3T. of the butter 2 minutes, turning once. Place in 350° oven 6-8 minutes.
2. While fish is in oven, sauté scallions, mushrooms and crabmeat in 3T. butter. Add chablis.
3. Blend bordelaise, remaining butter and lemon juice in a sauce pan. Lace serving plates with this sauce.
4. Place fillets on sauce and top with mushroom-crab mixture. Garnish with shredded spinach.

*See Glossary

Serves: 3-4

Preparation: 15 minutes

Cook: 10 minutes

"This is truly a magnificent fish preparation! !"

— NOTES —

LES MEDALLIONS DE VEAU CASIMIR
(Veal Casimir)

1½	lbs. veal scalloppine (pounded thin)
	flour for dusting
	salt and pepper to taste
¼	lb. butter for sautéing
¼	cup chablis
2	bananas (sliced ¼" diagonally into 32 pieces)
1	cup bordelaise*
½	cup béarnaise*
6	oz. whole Alaskan king crab legs (steamed and sliced lengthwise)

1. Salt and pepper veal. Dust lightly with flour.
2. Sauté veal in butter, 2 minutes each side. Remove, keep warm.
3. De-glaze* veal pan with chablis. Pour over veal. veal.
4. Sauté bananas in separate pan in butter.
5. Lace serving platter with bordelaise. Place veal on top. Nap with béarnaise. Run under broiler 2-3 minutes.
6. Arrange hot shrimp and crab on veal. Garnish border with bananas.

*See Glossary
Serves: 4
Preparation: 20 minutes
Cooking: 5-8 minutes

"Fond memories of this lovely entreé still linger. . .very rich but fabulous for that special dinner party."

NOISETTES OF LAMB WITH TARRAGON SAUCE
(Allow 20 Minutes to Make Tarragon Reduction)

1½   lb. lamb fillets about 1½ " thick
     salt and pepper
2   oz. butter
2   oz. frying oil
¼   cup chablis (white wine)
2   T. tarragon and wine reduction (See Note)
1½   cups bordelaise*
½   cup heavy cream

1.   Season fillets with salt and pepper. Sauté in butter and
     oil until done to your taste. Remove from pan and keep
     warm.
2.   De-glaze* pan with white wine. Add tarragon reduction,
     bordelaise and cream. Reduce* until creamy.
3.   To serve, nap fillets with sauce. Serve extra sauce on
     side.

*NOTE: Simmer 2 cups good red wine (Bordeaux) with
1 1/2 T. dry tarragon until it is 1/2 cup.

*See Glossary
Serves: 3-4
Preparation: 25 minutes
Cook: 8 minutes

"The subtle taste of lamb is complimented with this sauce! !"

– NOTES –

Raimondo's

coral gables

An interesting feature about Raimondo's is that chef-owner Raimondo Laudisio really looks like a chef. He's a large, rugged man dressed in white, with twinkling eyes and an enormous handlebar moustache. His culinary wizardly has made Raimondo's, located in Coral Gables, one of Miami's most popular Italian restaurants.

Featuring Northern Italian cuisine, the menu has an abundance of veal entrées but also includes luscious pasta, chicken, duck, lamb and beef.

Seafood is in abundance from *Scampi* to *Pompano in Cartoccio*, the freshest pompano baked in paper. *Veal Chops Tre Corone* are excellent as well as the *Veal Dante´ in Cartoccio*. Veal Dante is created with tender veal, ham and fresh Mozzarella and coated with bread and almond crumbs and lovingly baked. Try it with a refreshing *Hearts of Palm Salad* or one of *Belgian Endive*. A most enjoyable dessert would be fruit and cheese (with a light Chianti, of course) or a *Sabayon Souffl*é. Additional non-menu items are available from the blackboard according to present market conditions and Chef Raimondo's inspiration.

Raimondo's is a restaurant lavish in food but simple in decor. Rustic cypress paneling, tiffany style lamps, ceiling fans and hanging greenery create the aura of casualness. Large and colorful modern art livens the already cheery walls. But the real stars on parade are the multitude of savory and delicious dishes. Raimondo's has been a Travel/Holiday Magazine Award winner since 1973.

From the moment you arrive, heavenly aromas drifting from the kitchen at Raimondo's prepare you for the "Viva Italian" excellence of this superb experience. It is truly "Tutto Béné!"

Raimondo's was formerly located on 79th Street in Miami, but is now on LeJeune Road in Coral Gables. Take the Palmetto Expressway to Bird Road. Then go east on Bird to LeJeune, then south on LeJeune to 4612, which is almost at the intersection of LeJeune and Ponce De Leon. Raimondo's is on the right.

Reservations Necessary.

SPAGHETTI CARBONARA BERT

1	lb. spaghetti
3	T. butter
2	onions (chopped)
¼	lb. proscuitto or ham (julienne*)
1	cup grated Parmesan
1	cup chicken stock (or ½ cup cream, ½ cup stock)
4	egg yolks (beaten)
2	truffles with juice or ½ cup mushrooms (chopped)
	fresh ground pepper

1. Cook spaghetti al dente.* Drain and keep warm.
   warm.
2. Sauté onions in butter until golden. Add prosciutto and simmer. (If mushrooms are used, add with the prosciutto or ham.)
3. Quickly add spaghetti, stock, cheese, egg yolks. Toss well. Add truffles and pepper. Serve immediately.

*See Glossary
Serves: 4-6
Preparation: 15 minutes
Cooking: 15/10 minutes

"Always a welcome first or main course. Truffles add elegance!"

— NOTES —

VEAL CHOPS TRE CORONE

4	8 oz. veal loin chops
1/8	cup butter
1/8	cup olive oil
	salt and pepper to taste
4	shallots (chopped)
1	cup cepes (may be purchased at Gourmet Specialty Shops)
1	cup mushrooms (sliced)
½	cup vermouth
1	cup heavy cream
1	cup Fontina cheese (grated)
	dash of nutmeg
¼	t. sage
¼	t. rosemary (crushed)
1	T. butter
2	egg yolks (beaten)
	fresh ground pepper

1. Sauté chops in butter and oil on both sides until tender. Season with salt and pepper. Place on oven-proof platter to keep warm.
2. Sauté shallots, cepes and mushrooms. Place on chops.
3. Add vermouth to pan drippings and reduce* to 1T. Add cream, Fontina, nutmeg, sage and rosemary. Blend well.
4. Add 1 T. butter and beaten egg yolks. Season with salt and fresh ground pepper to taste. Spoon over chops to serve.

*See Glossary
Serves. 4
Preparation: 10 minutes
Cooking: 30 minutes

"The fine taste of Fontina enhances this veal dish!!"

miami

One of Miami's most visually dazzling restaurants is the ultra-modern Tuttle's at the Charter Club. Although named for one of the area pioneers, Julia Tuttle, it's certainly not shades of "the good old days" in decor. In electrifying chrome and glass, with accents of burgundy and gray, Tuttle's is a high-tech tour of the Twenty-First century.

Gleaming mirrors and Tivoli lights extend the vistas to infinity. Dining rooms are divided into intimate areas by burgundy velvet padded massive columns. Stark angles of chrome and glass tables are pillowed by the plush upholstered velvet of the chairs. Maroon and gray polka dot napkins complement the shimmering stemware. Touches of red oak and plants accent the stark modern decor and a view of the futuristic wine cellar commands center stage.

Cordon Bleu trained owner, Peter Whitcup, is understandably proud of Tuttle's. He is frequently seen in the kitchen while his lovely wife entertains diners at brunch or dinner with her melodic harp.

Indulge in *Duckling Melba, Scampi Florentine, Salmon Duglere* or *A Trio of Quail*, stuffed with pecans and mushrooms and served with truffled *Sauce Perigueux*. Delightful appetizers such as *Escargot Pot Pie* (snails in mushroom caps baked in a skillet with a puff pastry lid), add a slightly different twist to an old favorite. Forsake your diet with a dessert like the sensuously rich *Chocolate Millionaire*.

For the ultra ultimate in decor and affordable luxury in cuisine, the first choice among Miami's chic, young set is Tuttle's.

Tuttles is located at the Charter Club at 600 N.E. 36th Street. Take 95 south to 195-East. Before the causeway, exit on Biscayne Blvd. Turn south onto Biscayne Blvd., then west onto N.E. 36th Street, which is also Route 27. Tuttles is on the left side as you go west.

Reservations Suggested.

BIBB LETTUCE WITH HONEY AND LIME DRESSING
(Chill Plates & Forks in Freezer)

— SALAD —

4	small heads Bibb lettuce (washed thoroughly, well chilled and left whole to spread out like flowers)
6	oz. roasted Pistachios
8	oz. mandarin orange sections
	fresh mint (chopped)
1	cup honey-lime dressing (Recipe to follow)

1. Place individual lettuce heads on frozen plates. Lace with 2-3 oz. of honey-lime dressing.
2. Garnish with Pistachios, oranges and mint. Serve with frozen forks.

— HONEY-LIME DRESSING —

½	cup walnut oil (may be found in Gourmet Specialty Shops)
	zest* from 2 limes
¼	cup fresh lime juice
1/8	cup honey
1/8	cup shallots (chopped)
	salt and pepper to taste

1. Place all dressing ingredients in blender or food processor/emulsify.

Yield: 1 cup

*See Glossary
Serves: 4
Preparation: 10 minutes

"Exotic and refreshing! !"

FETTUCINE AL PESTO
(Make Pesto Butter Ahead)

— PESTO BUTTER —

1	stick butter (4 oz.)
1/8	cup (2T.) olive oil
1	clove garlic
¼	cup fresh basil or 2 t. dried
½	T. oregano
1/8	cup (2T.) white wine
2	T. pine nuts (ground)
1	T. parsley (chopped)
¼	t. sage
	salt and fresh ground pepper

— FETTUCINE —

½	lb. fettucine (cooked, shocked in cold water, drained)
	pesto butter
4	oz. raw shrimp
4	oz. raw bay scallops
4	oz. king crab
4	broccoli spears (cooked and drained)
12	green beans (cooked and drained)
2	oz. freshly grated Parmesan cheese
2	oz. pignolia nuts (pine nuts - found in Gourmet Specialty Shops)
	fresh ground pepper

— PESTO BUTTER —

1. Place all ingredients in a blender or food processor. Cream together about 5 minutes.

— FETTUCINE —

2. Place 4 oz. Pesto butter, shrimp, scallops, and king crab in a large skillet. Sauté until done.
3. Add fettucine, butter if necessary, toss. Add broccoli, beans, and cheese. Toss again.

-continued-

4. To serve, place tossed broccoli and beans on top. Sprinkle with pine nuts and fresh ground pepper. Pass extra cheese.

Serves: 4-6
Preparation: 25 minutes
Cooking: 10 minutes

"A hearty first course, or an entrée when adding more seafood and Pesto butter!!"

— NOTES —

CHOCOLATE MILLIONAIRE
(Allow Time to Chill)

6	oz. semi-sweet chocolate bits
¼	cup Grand Marnier
1/8	cup instant Sanka (powdered)
6	egg yolks
¼	cup sugar
1	pt. whipping cream (to be used in 8 oz. portions)
½	t. vanilla
	vanilla ice cream
	fresh strawberries
	Pistachios (chopped for garnish)
	mint sprigs (for garnish)

1. Make a mousse by melting chocolate bits with Grand Marnier in top of double boiler. Add powdered Sanka to hot chocolate mixture. Blend well.

2. Cream egg yolks and sugar in a mixer to obtain maximum volume. Add chocolate mixture and vanilla to this. Put in large bowl and refrigerate.

3. Without washing mixer bowl, whip one-half of the cream until maximum volume is attained. Fold into chocolate mixture until completely mixed. Refrigerate 2 hours.

4. To serve: Spoon mousse into 4 large stemmed glasses. Place scoop of ice cream on the mousse. Place several strawberries on top of that. Whip remaining half of the cream with a little Grand Marnier and place a dollop on each dessert. Garnish each with Pistachios and a sprig of mint.

Serves: 4-6
Preparation: 15 minutes
Chill: 2 hours

"The name says it all! !"

Vinton's

Wander the winding streets of Coral Gables and enjoy the Spanish style elegance of an almost forgotten time. Streets with names like Viscaya, Malaga, Catalonia and Majorca linger in the memory to evoke romantic images.

It is with such images in mind that one discovers Vinton's restaurant. Perhaps dinner will begin with *L'Avocat Maria Theresa* — an appetizer of avocado and King Crabmeat with Brandy Sauce or fresh *Beluga Caviar*. Entrées such as *Les Medallions de Veau Casimir* — veal scalloppine with crabmeat, shrimp and bananas suggest a tropical mood combined with French flair and elegance. Of course there are always truly special ways to conclude an evening at Vinton's — *Crêpes Suzette, Le Souffle' Glace Aux Framboises* (cold raspberry souffle), *Le Gateau Glace Marrakesh* (mocha ice cream cake with caramel sauce) are the creams de la Vinton's crop.

However, fine cuisine is not the only ingredient in Vinton's repertoire of delight. The setting is pure enchantment. Located in the old Spanish style Hotel La Palma, the mood is tropical. Visions of "Casablanca" arise at every turn. Potted palms, cool terrazzo floors, genuine old ceiling fans, white stucco walls, and graceful wicker Princess chairs set the mood. French doors open onto a courtyard of lush vegetation. Two other dining rooms are small and intimate — one with just three private and secluded tables in an alcove. The style is that of an old fashioned European parlor with heavy drapes, flowered carpeting and more subdued tones. Everywhere is the Vinton's trademark of white lace tablecloths over red. Fresh cut flowers grace tables and sideboards for a truly elegant effect!

Energetic, young owner, Hans Eichmann, along with co-worker and brother, René, speak with pride of their restaurant and its awards. United Mainliner, Golden Spoon, Travel/ Holiday Magazine and Miami Magazine — to name just a few. They're also justly proud of the other Vinton's restaurant, Vinton's New Orleans in Lake Wales. Its owner is Nettie Davis who is Hans' mother-in-law.

Both Vinton's New Orleans in Lake Wales and Vinton's in Coral Gables are proof that successful restaurants are often a family affair.

To find Vinton's Town House, take the Palmetto Expressway south to S.W. 40th Street (Bird Road), then go east on Bird Road to LeJeune Road. Head north on LeJeune Road to Coral Way, then east on Coral Way to Ponce De Leon Blvd. Then proceed north on Ponce De Leon Blvd. to Alhambra Circle. Vinton's is on the corner of Alhambra and Galiano in the Hotel La Palma.

Reservations Suggested.

GROUPER A'LA CHEF RENÉ

2½-3 lbs. grouper fillets
½ cup flour for dusting
½ cup oil for frying

— BATTER —
4 eggs
1 cup beer
2 cups flour
   salt and pepper to taste

— SAUCE RENÉ —
1 cup butter
1 cup tomatoes (peeled and diced)
½ cup onions (chopped)
1/3 cup capers
1/8 cup parsley (chopped)
1 cup white wine
   salt and pepper to taste

— GARNISH —
1/3 cup toasted sliced almonds
   chopped parsley
   lemon wedges

— BATTER —
1. Beat eggs. Add beer, salt and pepper. Mix into flour until smooth. Refrigerate for 30 minutes.

— SAUCE —
2. Melt butter in sauce pan. Add tomatoes, onions, capers and parsley. Simmer 5 minutes leaving onions firm. Add wine and seasonings. Keep warm.

-continued-

— FILLETS —

3. Dust fillets in flour. Dip completely in batter. Shake off excess batter. Brown lightly in a good oil. Bake in 400° oven until cooked and crisp.

4. Place on serving platter. Cover entirely with SAUCE RENÉ. Sprinkle with almonds and parsley. Garnish with lemon wedges.

Serves: 6
Preparation: 40 minutes
Cooking: 10/15 minutes

"Wonderful grouper in a great light sauce!"

— NOTES —

OYSTER AND LOBSTER, CUISINE NOUVELLE

4-6 Maine lobsters or Florida lobster tails
12-15 oysters (shucked)
1 carrot (julienne)*
1 leek (julienne)
2 T. butter
4 shallots
1 T. oil
2 oz. brandy
1 bunch parsley (½ chopped, ½ for garnish)
1½ cups whipping cream
salt and pepper to taste
4 T. butter (2 oz.)

1. Parboil lobster tails. Remove meat. Cut in cubes and set aside.
2. Sauté carrots and leeks in 2 T. butter for 2 minutes. Remove from pan.
3. Sauté shallots in 1 T. oil in same pan for 2 minutes.
4. Add lobster cubes and oysters. Stir until seared. Remove contents from pan.
5. Flame residue carefully with brandy. Add chopped parsley and cream. Season with salt and pepper and reduce.*
6. Add 4 T. butter and stir until smooth and creamy.
7. Add lobster and oysters. Simmer 1 minute.
8. To serve, pour on serving plate. Sprinkle julienne vegetables on top. Garnish with parsley sprigs.

*See Glossary
Serves: 6
Preparation: 15 minutes
Cooking: 10/10 minutes

"Great and unusual seafood dish!"

Le SOUFFLÉ GLACÉ AUX FRAMBOISES
(Cold Raspberry Souffle)

4	pints fresh raspberries (or 2 packages frozen)
1	cup sugar
2	cups whipping cream
2	egg yolks (beaten)
3	egg whites (beaten)
2	T. sugar

— GARNISH —
fresh mint leaves
shaved chocolate

1. In a sauce pan cook raspberries and sugar until thick. (If using frozen berries delete sugar)
2. Push mixture through strainer to remove seeds. Cool.
3. Whip cream in a large bowl. Add cool raspberry syrup reserving 6 t. Mix in egg yolks.
4. Beat egg whites until shiney. Add 2T. sugar slowly, beat again.
5. Whip egg whites into raspberry-cream mixture gently until smooth.
6. Pour into soufflé dishes that have been extended with collars to enhance soufflé effect.
7. Place in freezer until firm but not frozen.
8. Serve each soufflé topped with 1 t. reserved syrup, mint leaves and shaved chocolate.

Serves: 4-6
Preparation: 20 minutes
Cooking: 10 minutes for raspberries

"Elegant raspberry flavor in a pretty dessert!"

The Captain's Table Restaurant
Cedar Key, Fla.

Visitors to Florida are obsessed by sun worshiping, frolicking in our salty waters, and visiting as many attractions as possible along their way. But some of our finest attractions are those least publicized, and most pleasurable. Tucked away along Florida's varied coastline, you'll find the most intriguing restaurants. Cedar Key's famous Captain's Table Restaurant attracts locals and visitors alike to savor the succulent seafood.

A bit off the beaten track, on the Gulf of Mexico, Cedar Key is well worth the detour. Just southwest of Gainesville, Florida residents venture hundreds of miles to dine at this casual waterfront abode. Be careful while traveling into the Key at night as the road leading into this quaint fishing village is virtually lightless!

Friendly owners Helen and Ray Brown have operated their homey restaurant for over a decade. As Helen tells the story, when they opened the doors in 1971, she started serving the kind of seafood she had been taught to cook by her grandmother, known to Cedar Key residents as Aunt Rivvie Hathcox. Husband Ray built the restaurant which originally would seat only 75 persons. Today the restaurant has doubled in size to accommodate the large crowd who regularly await Helen's luscious cuisine.

I waited a few minutes to talk with Helen, when she briefly surfaced, sleeves rolled up, to chat. She explained that she was in the midst of creating her Island Lime Pies and apologized for being unable to spend more time with me. An animated woman who obviously speaks her mind, she related how her love of cooking and drive to keep busy helped her to achieve the successful Captain's Table. Modestly, she admits,

"My experience in cooking and preparing seafood for the restaurant was gained by working eight years for Bessie Gibbs, and the advice of Webster Johnson, another local resident who was famous for his cuisine. Some of these recipes and ideas in serving seafood were given to me by them."

The "Captain's Table" is built on an historic spot, the exact location where a railroad track leading into the town to ship seafood, terminated. The restaurant now stands on these beginnings of the first cross-state railroad in Florida.

Old photographs of Cedar Key, fishermen's nets and artifacts brought in by the local anglers, including stuffed fish, add a rustic tint to this famous restaurant. The view of Sea Horse Island and the surrounding waterways is breathtaking!

Enjoy the *Oysters Wrapped in Bacon*, tiny blue *Crab Fingers* or the generous seafood platters consisting of fish, crab, shrimp, oysters and scallops. *Stuffed Flounder* and *Deviled Crab* are the most popular with the townsfolk.

For years, I have visited "The Captain's Table" and enjoyed the sumptuous seafood. One of my favorites has always been the *Hearts of Palm Salad* with lettuce, shredded hearts of palm, papaya, banana and pineapple chunks all topped with lime sherbet dressing and dates. An unparalleled creation.

Since the old "White House Hotel" was in business on the top of the hill across from the Baptist Church, Cedar Key has been famous for its fresh and well prepared seafood. We think you'll agree after sampling these fabulous recipes.

To reach The Captain's Table, take U.S. 19 to Otter Creek and head west. Follow State Road 24 to Cedar Key to the Pier. The Captain's Table is located on the Pier.

HEARTS OF PALM SALAD WITH SHERBET DRESSING
(Dressing Can Be Made Ahead and Frozen)

1	can hearts of palm (sliced)
2	papayas (peeled and cubed)
2	bananas (sliced)
1	fresh pineapple (cubes or 1 can of chunks)
1	small box of dates (chopped)
1	pt. frozen sherbet dressing (Recipe to follow)

— FROZEN SHERBET DRESSING —

1	pt. lime sherbet
1	pt. pineapple sherbet
¼	cup mayonnaise
7	oz. extra-crunchy peanut butter
3	oz. real lemon juice
	a drop or two of green food coloring

— DRESSING —

1. Soften sherbet while mixing mayonnaise, peanut butter and lemon juice together.
2. Whip peanut butter mixture in with sherbet. Return to freezer until ready to serve.

— SALAD —

3. Mix fruits together and serve on individual lettuce lined plates. Top with a scoop of frozen dressing.

Serves: 6-8
Preparation: 20 minutes

"A cool and tropical favorite! !"

— NOTES —

BAKED STUFFED RED FISH

1½	lbs. red fish or trout (leave whole)
½	box Stove Top Stuffing (chicken flavored)
½	lb. crab meat
½	can cream of mushroom soup
1	onion sliced
½	cup white wine
	butter
	paprika

1. Mix cooked stuffing, crabmeat and soup. Stuff inside cleaned fish.
2. Put onions and wine in a buttered baking dish. Place fish on top. Butter the fish and sprinkle with paprika.
3. Bake in 350° oven for 45 minutes, or microwave 4-8 minutes.

Serves: 3
Preparation: 20 minutes
Cooking: 45 minutes or 4-8 minutes in microwave

"Everyone loves this. . .fillets of any white fish may be used with stuffing in between! !"

— NOTES —

ISLAND LIME PIE

2	cans condensed milk
1	cup lime juice
½	cup lemon juice
2	egg yolks (beaten)
1	9" graham cracker crumb crust

1. Mix all ingredients with electric mixer.
2. Pour into cracker crust and freeze.
3. Top with Dream Whip and leave in freezer until ready to eat.

Serves: 8
Preparation: 15 minutes
Freeze until ready to use

"Freezing the pie enhances the lime flavor of this creamy delight!"

—NOTES —

Chalet Suzanne®

RESTAURANT AND COUNTRY INN

lake wales

The Chalet Suzanne Country Inn and Restaurant is a delightful mix of jumbled gingerbread architecture, housing priceless objects d'art collected by the founder Bertha Hinshaw. Her son, Carl, now runs the inn and restaurant, assisted by his wife Vita, and children Tina and Eric. Their group efforts enable Chalet Suzanne to do such things as: produce its own line of gourmet soups available to the public, be a consistent winner of the Florida Trend Golden Spoon, Mobil Four Star and Holiday Fine Dining Awards, and continually satisfy faithful patrons of the Lake Wales area.

The most striking feature of Chalet Suzanne is the restaurant decor. In each of the five dining rooms, animated by cheerful waitresses in "Heidi" outfits, every tile table is set with different china and different silver patterns. In addition, there is a fascinating hodge-podge of antique chairs from every conceivable period. This interior decorating scheme has been a tremendous success. Perhaps the reason being, that you are continually stimulated by unique changes in scenery wherever you turn. From the lively dining rooms to the colorful guest rooms, the Chalet Suzanne is a unique experience. What other inn would offer guests a "banana" to sleep in? ("Banana" is a guest room decorated in shades of ripe, vibrant, yellow.)

Fortunately for us there's no whimsy or frivolity in the Hinshaw's dedication to fine cuisine! Your first bite of tender, succulent *Crab with Herb Butter* or flaky delicate *Potato Rolls*, is as stimulating to your taste buds as the decor is enchanting to your eyes. Try the *Soup Romaine,*® regulars insist you start your meal with this favorite.

The Chalet Suzanne is located in central Florida in an area yet unspoiled by a city pace. The area's charm, beauty and down-home hospitality are perfectly depicted by this restaurant's genteel service and excellent food.

Chalet Suzanne is located between U.S. 27 and Alternate 27 on Masterpiece Road (17A). From I-4, go south on U.S. 27 until 17A and take a left onto Masterpiece Road. From the town of Lake Wales, go north on U.S. 27 until 17A, then take a right onto 17A. It's less than a mile to Chalet Suzanne.

Reservations Suggested.

ROQUEFORT MOUSSE DEAN
(Allow 2-3 Hours to Chill)

1½	envelopes unflavored gelatin (1½T.)
¼	cup cold water
6	egg yolks
2	cups whipping cream
¾	lb. Roquefort
3	egg whites (stiffly beaten)
2	T. poppy seeds

1. Sprinkle gelatin over cold water to soften.
2. Combine egg yolks and 1/2 cup cream in a heavy sauce pan. Over low heat, cook and whisk until mixture is creamy and slightly thickened.
3. Add gelatin and beat until dissolved. Pour into a large mixing bowl and set aside.
4. Process cheese in a blender or food processor until smooth, and add to gelatin mixture. Cool until partially set.
5. Whip remaining cream and fold into cheese mixture. Then fold in egg whites and poppy seeds.
6. Pour into a 2-qt. oiled mold and chill until firm. Unmold on serving plate, garnish and serve with crudités, toast rounds and crackers.

Serves: 35 for hors d'oeuvres
Preparation: 20 minutes
Chill: 2-3 hours

"Light and different appetizer! !"
— NOTES —

BAKED GRAPEFRUIT

½   grapefruit per person
     butter (melted)
     sugar
     cinnamon
     chicken livers
     flour
     salt
     pepper
     butter

1. Cut out small center of each grapefruit half and loosen sections.
2. Fill center cavity with melted butter. Sprinkle top with a mixture of cinnamon and sugar. (Generously!)
3. Place under broiler until well browned.
4. To serve, garnish with a chicken liver or two that have been dusted with flour, salt and pepper and sautéed on a hot grill or skillet in butter.

Serves: 1
Preparation: 4 minutes

"An easy but favorite first course in Florida! (They say Baked Grapefruit originated at the Chalet Suzanne.)"

— NOTES —

SEAFOOD-MUSHROOM SOUP WITH SHERRY

6	T. butter
9	T. flour
2	cups milk
3	cups light cream
1½	cups seafood (chopped and cooked): one or a combination of cod, haddock, lobster and shrimp.
½	cup mushrooms (sliced and sautéed in 1T. butter)
1	hard cooked egg (chopped)
½	t. grated lemon rind
1	T. salt (or to taste)
¼	t. white pepper
½	t. sugar
4	T. Harvey's Bristol Cream Sherry
3	hard cooked egg yolks (sieved for garnish)
2	T. chives (chopped for garnish)

1. Melt butter in top of double boiler. Add flour and stir with a whisk until well blended.
2. Add milk and cream, stirring until mixture simmers.
3. Add remaining ingredients except for sherry, and cook 25 minutes.
4. Add sherry 5 minutes before serving. Pour into soup bowls and garnish with egg yolk and chives.

Serves: 6
Preparation: 15 minutes
Cooking: 35 minutes

"Rich but delicate! !"

— NOTES —

GÂTEAU CHRISTINA
(Allow 24 Hours to Refrigerate)

— MERINGUE —

4   egg whites
1½ cups sugar
1/3 cup blanched almonds (ground)

— CHOCOLATE FILLING —

2   egg whites
½   cup sugar
2   T. sweetened cocoa
1   cup butter (softened)
4   oz. semi-sweet chocolate (melted)

— MERINGUE —

1. Preheat oven to 250°. Cut 4 rounds of foil about 8" in diameter. Place on cookie sheet and grease them.
2. Whip egg whites until stiff, gradually adding sugar, as eggs begin to hold their shape. Then add almonds.
3. Spread meringue on foil rounds with rubber spatula, leaving ½" around edge. Bake 15-25 minutes or until meringue is dry.(Baking time will vary depending on humidity and individual oven.)
4. Turn meringues over and peel foil off carefully. Bake 5 minutes more.

— CHOCOLATE FILLING —

5. In top of double boiler over hot water (not boiling), beat egg whites until foamy.
6. Gradually add and whisk: sugar, cocoa, butter and melted chocolate. Beat until thick and creamy. Remove from heat and allow to cool.

— TO ASSEMBLE GATEAU —

7. Reserve some filling for icing top. Place best meringue layer on bottom and spread with filling. Top with

-continued-

another meringue, press lightly, allowing meringue to crack in order to conform to lower layer. Cracking is alright as filling will hold layers together. Repeat process until all meringues are used. Carefully spread reserved filling on top and refrigerate for a least 24 hours.

Serves: 8-10
Preparation and Cooking: 30-45 minutes
Refrigerate: 24 hours

"One of the best chocolate sauces we've tasted. As a filling with meringues this is most impressive! May be made with smaller meringue circles for individual Gateaux."

The Empress Lilly Riverboat

© 1981 Walt Disney Productions

The Empress Room

Empress Lilly Riverboat
Walt Disney World Village
At Lake Buena Vista

A sophisticated lady graces the lovely shoreline of Lake Buena Vista in Walt Disney World Village, with the casual radiance of a reigning beauty queen.

This lady is The Empress Lilly, a 220 - foot long permanently moored paddlewheeler, that proudly features the finest in dining, in her three lovely restaurants. We visited The Empress Room, the most elegant of the trio.

For a delightful evening and the most exclusive in formal French service, The Empress Room is a prime choice. Maria Theresa Chandeliers grace the sparkling decor, a most sophisticated Louis XV setting. Freshly cut pink roses bedeck the impeccable snow white linen service. Gold inlay china, in the fairest of rose tones, along with etched glass accents and brilliant satins create a most harmonious setting. An enchanting atmosphere, that magically turns any occasion into a very special occasion!

A large gold menu is masterfully done, but the real wealth lies within. Executive Chef Garry Reich allows no detail to go unattended. Recipient of the Florida Trend Golden Spoon Award, the restaurant can proudly boast of its amicable Hungarian Chef, who has been employed by such notables as President Lyndon Johnson and Howard Hughes.

For an enchanting appetizer, sample the *Les Huîtres Sautées En Barquette*, buttery sautéed oysters with garlic-wine butter. Soups are fabulous and include *Veloute d'Epinard et d'Huîtres*, a Spinach and Oyster Soup and *La Crème Vichyssoise d'Avocat*, a chilled avocado soup served in specially molded ice. And the ultimate dining experience continues with such expertly created dishes as *La Saumon Poché dans Court Bouillon*, poached salmon with Mousseline Sauce. The *Les Trois Lilly*, a trio of center cuts of lamb, veal and wild boar are três elegante! The sumptuous meals are in keeping with the customary feasts of riverboat elite in the 1880's. . .each a worldly experience.

Our visit to The Empress was a most impressive, romantic dining experience. . .She is the *Love Boat* of the river, a majestic masterpiece of authenticity, and a regal queen.

How to find the Empress Room: Follow the signs from Interstate 4 at Exit 535 to Walt Disney World Village, Lake Buena Vista.

Reservations Necessary.

L'EMINCE de FILET à la TARTARE
Sliced Steak Tartare

---

3   1 oz. slices beef filet (pounded as thin as possible)

— DRESSING —
1   cup salad oil
¼   cup red wine vinegar
½   cup capers (chopped fine)
1/8 cup shallots (chopped fine)
1   anchovy (minced)
1   t. Worchestershire sauce
     salt and pepper to taste

— GARNISH —
     Lettuce leaves
1   hard cooked egg (chopped)
¼   cup parsley (chopped)
3   cherry tomatoes (optional)
3   small pickles (optional)

1.   Mix all dressing ingredients well — Keep chilled.

— GARNISH —

2.   To serve, (on chilled plates) place filets on lettuce leaves. Sprinkle with chopped eggs and parsley. Garnish with tomatoes and pickles.
3.   Serve dressing on the side, so guests may take as much as desired.

Serves: 3
Preparation: 10 minutes

"A different way to serve this classic appetizer!"

LES HUÎTRES SAUTÉES en BARQUETTE
Sauteed Oysters, With Garlic-Wine Butter

1	loaf unsliced bread
30	oysters (5 for each serving)
	salt and pepper to taste
	flour
2	eggs (beaten and strained)
	fresh bread crumbs (from loaf)
2	T. butter
	white wine butter (Recipe to follow)

1. Trim crust from bread to form eight-sided loaf. Slice into six equal 2" slices. Cut out center to make a basket called a "barquette." Toast until very hard.
2. Drain oysters, salt and pepper, and lightly dredge in flour. Dip in egg and coat evenly with bread crumbs.
3. Sauté oysters in small amount of butter, until golden brown. Place five in each barquette. Pour White Wine Butter over barquette. Saturate.

— WHITE WINE BUTTER —

2	t. garlic (minced)
2	t. shallots (minced)
2	lbs. butter
2	cups white wine (sauterne)
2	t. Worchestershire sauce
2	T. parsley chopped

4. Lightly sauté garlic and shallots in small amount of butter. Add wine and reduce by 1/3. Add butter and melt. Add Worchestershire sauce and parsley.

Serves: 6
Preparation: 20 minutes
Cooking: 15 minutes

"This is a rich and heavenly first course! ! Every superlative is well deserved!"

LA CRÈME VICHYSSOISE d' AVOCAT
Cold Avocado Soup (Allow time to chill)

1	whole leek (cleaned and diced)
½	cup celery (diced)
½	onion (chopped)
2	potatoes (peeled and quartered)
1	qt. chicken broth
1-2	ripe avocados (cubed)
1-2	cups heavy cream
	butter for sautéing
6	drops Worchestershire sauce
	salt and white pepper to taste
	chopped chives (for garnish)

1. Sauté leeks, celery and onions in butter.
2. Add potatoes, chicken stock and salt. Simmer until potatoes are done. Cool completely.
3. Purée mixture with 1-2 avocados. Strain through very fine strainer or cheese cloth.
4. Stir in 1-2 cups of cream, as desired. Add Worchestershire and white pepper. Taste for salt. Chill until very cold. Serve in frozen cups. Garnish with chopped chives.

Serves: 8
Preparation: 10 minutes
Cooking: 30 minutes

"We preferred using two avocados because of their wonderful flavor. The Empress Room serves this in ramekins, inserted in molded ice. A very impressive display! !"

— NOTES —

LES POIS MANGE - TOUT et RADIS BLANC
Pea Pod Salad with Lemon/Ginger Dressing
(Chill Plates Ahead)

12-14	oz. fresh pea pods (3½oz. per serving)
3-4	white radishes (cleaned and sliced thin)
	Salt to taste

— DRESSING —

1½	T. fresh ginger (minced)
2	shallots (minced)
2½	oz. lemon juice
1	egg yolk
	salt and pepper to taste
1	t. sugar
¼	cup olive oil
¾	cup salad oil
½	cup red wine vinegar
1	t. Worcestershire sauce

1. Pick off ends of pea pods. Blanche in boiling salted water for 40 seconds. Cool in ice immediately.
2. Mix pea pods with radishes.

— DRESSING —

3. Soak ginger and shallots in lemon juice. (put aside)
4. Mix egg yolk with salt, pepper and sugar.
5. Slowly blend in oils and vinegar. Add lemon/ginger mixture. Stir in Worcestershire. Chill.
6. Toss peapods and radishes with dressing. Serve on frozen plates.

Yield: 2 cups

Serves: 4
Preparation: 15 minutes
Chill

"Light and refreshing with any meal. A perfect answer for a chinese menu!"

Klaus'
CUISINE

daytona beach

At the very top of Klaus' menu is printed a French proverb which reads, "To invite anyone to dinner implies that we charge ourselves with his happiness all the time he is under our roof". Klaus and Barbara Friedenreich, proprietors of this famous restaurant do this to the utmost!

One would probably expect central Florida to have a number of excellent restaurants with good chefs. But I was most pleased to find a gourmet restaurant owned by an internationally recognized chef, Klaus Friedenreich.

Captain of the National 1980 U.S. Olympic Culinary Team at the International Culinary Olympics, Klaus won three gold medals. Part of the winning "hot food", was his extraordinary Turkey Breast Oklahoma. Klaus is also a member of the Honorary Order of the Golden Togue, (a professional organization limited to 100 lifetime members worldwide) and along with wife Barbara, the *Chaine Des Rotisseurs*.

Klaus' is a small restaurant seating only 150, though mirrors on the back wall make the one multi-level room appear much larger. The huge Cimbali Expresso machine is the focal point of the room. The classy Key West decor, ceiling fans and oversized wicker chairs lend a most casual effect. Oversized wine goblets and bamboo styled water glasses are unique to this restaurant. Fresh flowers and ferns complete the enchanting decor.

Entrées include *Tournedos Connoisseur*, twin fillets topped with fresh mushroom caps and served with rich bordelaise and béarnaise. For an appetizer try such delights as *Escargot Chabilisienne* bathed in chablis and simmered in herb and garlic butters. For lighter appetites, try the *Klaus' Quiche*, *Shrimp Bisque* or the luscious *Strawberry Soup*. Entrées are served with homemade cheese spread, vegetable plate with dip and the most delectable popovers ever! (Do they make them anywhere else in Florida? ! !)

The Expresso Machine invites you to try ten different kinds varying from plain to *Klaus' Cappucino,* a special concoction of three liqueurs topped with heavy whipped cream. And for dessert, the *Apple Cheese Torte* will give you something to talk about for weeks with its rich buttery crust filled with cream cheese and topped with sliced apples and almonds.

A visit to Daytona necessitates a visit to this most masterful restaurant!

Klaus' cuisine in Holly Hills is located 1 block north of Daytona Beach at 144 Ridgewood (U.S. 1).

Reservations Suggested.

STRAWBERRY SOUP

1	pt. strawberries (cleaned and hulled)
1	cup sour cream
½	cup milk
½	cup ginger ale
6	T. sugar
1	t. vanilla
1	T. lemon juice
	whole strawberries (sliced for garnish)

1. Combine all ingredients in a blender or food processor. Blend until smooth, chill well.
2. Serve in frozen cups. Garnish with strawberry slices.

Serves: 6
Preparation: 10 minutes

"An intriguing soup course! !"

— NOTES —

KLAUS' REUBEN
(Preheat oven 350º)

½   slice rye bread
1   9x9x1/8" thick puff pastry
     (available in frozen food section of super market, Pepperidge Farm brand.)
3   oz. lean corned beef (thinly sliced)
2   oz. sauerkraut (well drained)
1   T. thousand island dressing
1   oz. swiss cheese (sliced)
1   egg (beaten)

1. Place bread in center of puff pastry. Top with beef, sauerkraut, dressing and cheese.
2. Brush corners of pastry with beaten egg. Fold over filling and brush top with egg.
3. Bake 350º for 20 minutes or until done and golden brown.

Serves: 1
Preparation: 10 minutes
Cook: 20 minutes

"An elegant touch to an already great sandwich! !"

— NOTES —

NEW ENGLAND PORK CUTLET

6   boneless pork chops (butterflied)
1   egg (beaten)

— STUFFING —
3   cups apples (peeled, cored and chopped)
½   cup raisins
½   t. curry powder
     butter

— BREADING —
2   cups fresh bread crumbs
½   cup walnuts (finely chopped)

— STUFFING —
1. Sauté stuffing ingredients in butter.

— CUTLET —
2. Pound pork to 1/4" thick.
3. Brush edges of each pork cutlet with egg. Place 1/2 cup stuffing in chop and fold over. Press edges to seal.
4. Roll in breading mixture. Sauté in butter until golden brown. Bake in oven 350° for 10 minutes.

Serves: 6
Preparation: 15 minutes
Cooking: 20 minutes

"A memorable change of pace for pork!"

TURKEY BREAST OKLAHOMA*

**WINNING RECIPE OF THE
UNITED STATES CULINARY TEAM
1980 INTERNATIONAL CULINARY
COMPETITION - FRANKFURT, GERMANY**

*As submitted to Kraft Foodservice
by the 1980 U.S. Culinary Team

— FORCED MEAT —

1½	lbs. white raw turkey meat
4	oz. fat back (unsalted salt pork - diced)
1	egg
1	t. salt to taste
½	t. pepper to taste
5	oz. dark raw turkey meat, (cut in julienne strips)
½	stick butter (for basting)

— STUFFING —

¾	cup onions (chopped)
2	cloves garlic, minced
¾	cup carrots (diced)
½	cup parsley stems (chopped)
1/3	cup butter
½	lb. mushrooms (diced)
3	oz. Virginia ham (ham)
3	green onions, (sliced)
½	t. sage, to taste
½	t. thyme
	liver and giblets from turkey - cooked and diced (approximately 3 oz.)
2	egg yolks (beaten)
1½	cups coarse bread crumbs
	salt and pepper to taste
3	T. butter

-continued-

— FORCED MEAT —

1. Grind white meat and fat back in food processor. Blend in egg, salt and pepper. Fold in dark meat.
2. Spread on plastic wrap (placed on cookie sheet) about 9" X 12" and 1/4" thick. Refrigerate.

— STUFFING —

3. Sauté onions, garlic, carrots and parsley in butter. Add mushrooms, ham, green onions, sage, thyme and continue to sauté.
4. Add liver and giblets. Remove from heat. Add eggs and bread crumbs. Blend and season with salt and pepper. Cool.

— TO MAKE ROLL —

5. Spread stuffing on top of forced layer, being careful not to spread to edges.
6. Roll jelly-roll fashion, removing plastic wrap as you roll. Pat smooth with water and seal ends.
7. Bake in roasting pan 1-1 1/2 hours at 375°, basting 4 times with 1/2 stick butter and drippings. Slice for serving.

Serves: 6-8
Preparation: 45 minutes
Cooking: 1-1 1/2 hours

"Now - this is impressive! ! An elegant and great tasting entrée!"

— NOTES —

APPLE CHEESE TORTE

— CRUST —
½   cup butter (softened)
1/3   cup sugar
¼   t. vanilla
1   cup flour

— FILLING —
8   oz. cream cheese (softened)
¼   cup sugar
1   egg
½   t. vanilla

— TOPPING —
1/3   cup sugar
½   t. cinnamon
4   cups apples (approx. 4 apples/peeled & sliced)
¼   cup sliced almonds
      fresh whipped cream (for garnish)

— CRUST —
1. Cream butter, sugar and vanilla. Blend in flour.
2. Spread dough into bottom and up 1/2 the sides of a 9" spring form pan.

— FILLING —
3. Cream together cheese and sugar. Add egg and vanilla. Mix well and pour into pastry-lined pan.

— TOPPING —
4. Combine sugar and cinnamon. Toss apples in this mixture.
5. Spoon apples over cheese layer. Sprinkle with almonds.
6. Bake at 450° for 10 minutes. Reduce heat to 400° and continue baking for 25 minutes. Cool before removing from pan.

-continued-

7. May be served with a dollop of whipped cream.

Serves: 8
Preparation: 20 minutes
Cooking: 35 minutes

"This is easier to prepare than it looks and well worth it. A pie pan may be used if you don't have a spring form. Do not let the pastry show above the apple layer."

— NOTES —

Maison & Jardin
Restaurant

Pristine white in a grove of trees and looking like some-one's perfectly elegant villa — that's Maison & Jardin in Altamonte Springs. Interior courtyards, classical sculpture, oriental rugs and antiques give a feeling of timeless beauty and unhurried elegance. The grounds surrounding this lovely "maison" were once part of a thousand acre hunting retreat. That country feeling still remains and the well cared for "jardin" reminds patrons of the old world delight in nature's beauty.

This serenity and peacefulness are quite a contrast to the energetic, vibrant personality of owner William Beuret, Jr. Both he and his father, William Beuret, Sr., are deeply involv-ed in the day to day operation of Maison & Jardin and have been since they acquired the restaurant in 1972. It wasn't long after that Maison & Jardin began to garner such awards as the Holiday Fine Dining Award, Florida Trend Magazine's Gold Spoon and Mobil Guide Four Star.

Varied menu selections such as *Entrecote Foyots,* New York strip steak with the richest bearnaise sauce you've ever tasted, *Veal Chops Palace,* veal chops stuffed with oysters and wild rice, and *Truite au Champagne,* stuffed rainbow trout with champagne sauce plus many other selections enable guests to experience the art of fine dining Maison & Jardin style. . . and that's quite a lot of style!

Maison & Jardin is located at 430 Wymore Road in Altamonte Springs. At the intersection of I-4 and State Road 436, exit and turn west. At the second light turn south onto Wymore Road, and in less than a mile Maison & Jardin's sign will be visible.

Reservations Suggested.

FRESH CITRUS SOUP

3	oranges
3	grapefruits
1	cup sugar
¼	cup water
½	cup currant jelly
2	T. brandy
	sour cream

1. From the rind of the fruits, make julienne* strips for garnish.
2. Peel the fruit and cut out the sections carefully, removing pits and seeds. Cut grapefruit sections into smaller pieces. Place all in a bowl.
3. Cook the sugar, water and jelly 15 minutes to make a syrup. Cool.
4. Pour syrup over orange and grapefruit sections. Add brandy, stir and chill.
5. To serve, pour in cups and top with dollops of sour cream. Garnish with julienne strips.

*See Glossary
Serves: 8
Preparation: 25 minutes
Chill: 2-3 hours

"A favorite in Florida! !"

— NOTES —

FLAMING SPINACH SALAD
(*A Specialté of the House)

2	large handfuls of fresh spinach
4	slices of bacon
	red wine vinegar (enough to equal just less than drippings from bacon)
1	t. Worcestershire sauce
1	T. sugar
	juice from ½ lemon
2	T. brandy

1. Thoroughly wash, clean and stem spinach. Break in pieces.
2. In small pan, sauté bacon until just before crisp. Cut bacon in pieces.
3. Add wine vinegar to drippings. Stir, add Worcestershire and sugar. Simmer.
4. Sprinkle lemon juice over spinach in a bowl. Pour dripping mixture over and toss until well coated, leaving bacon in pan.
5. When bacon is thoroughly crisp, remove from heat and flame carefully with warmed brandy. Spoon over spinach and serve immediately.

Serves: 2
Preparation: 10 minutes
Cooking: 10 minutes

"A deliciously different spinach salad."

— NOTES —

FRESH TROUT WITH LIME BUTTER

fresh water trout (12 oz.)
salt
pepper
Lea & Perrin Sauce
lime juice
flour **(Add measure of ingredients to your own taste.)**
melted butter
juice of 1 lime
parsley (chopped)
fluted lime.

1. Season trout with salt, pepper, Lea & Perrin and lime juice.
2. Dip in flour and coat lightly on both sides.
3. In a hot sauté pan, add melted butter and trout. Cook on each side for approximately four minutes or until golden brown and cooked.
4. Place fish on hot plate, reserving butter from pan.
5. Add lime juice to butter and bring to a boil. Pour over trout.
6. Sprinkle chopped parsley over fish and garnish with fluted lime.

Serves: 1
Preparation: 5 minutes
Cooking: 8 minutes

"A simple but elegant entrée."

— NOTES —

VEAL STRASSBOURG WITH MOREL SAUCE

— VEAL —

12	3 oz. veal cutlets (pounded thin)
6	oz. pâté de foie gras
	salt
	pepper
	flour
	butter
1	quart Morel Sauce (Recipe to follow)

— MOREL SAUCE —

(Soak morels or mushrooms 1 hour)

2	oz. dried morels (dried wild European mushrooms may be substituted)
1-2	T. butter
2	T. shallots (chopped)
1	quart whipping cream
1	T. meat glaze (may be found in Gourmet Specialty Shops)
2	T. roux*
	salt and pepper to taste

— MOREL SAUCE —

1. Soak morels or mushrooms in water 1/2 hour. Drain and repeat in fresh water. Wash again if necessary to remove all grit. Cut in half or in smaller pieces. Drain well.
2. Sauté morels in butter, as hot as possible without burning.
3. Add shallots, brandy and carefully flame.
4. Add cream, stirring and reduce* for 10 minutes. *
5. Add meat glaze and roux. Season with salt and white pepper. Cook and stir 15 minutes. Yield: 1 quart. Set aside.

— VEAL —

6. Spread pâté evenly over six veal cutlets. Top with remaining six, gently pressing together. -continued-

7. Sprinkle with salt and pepper. Dredge in flour, (may be done ahead at this point and refrigerated.)
8. Sauté in butter, (about 3 minutes for each side.)
9. To serve, pour Morel Sauce over each portion and garnish. Serve remaining sauce on the side.

*See Glossary
Serves: 6
Preparation: 15 minutes
Cooking: 6-8 minutes

"Wonderfully continental!. . . A rich flavor!"

— NOTES —

MOCCA JAVA PIE

— PIE —

1   9" graham cracker crust (homemade, baked and sprinkled with brandy.)
1   quart coffee brandy ice cream (softened slightly)
½   cup pecan pieces
1½ cups chocolate fudge sauce (Recipe to follow)
     whipped cream

— CHOCOLATE FUDGE SAUCE —

2½ squares unsweetened Hershey's chocolate
¼   cup butter
1½ cups confectioner's powdered sugar
7/8 cup light cream
1   t. vanilla (not imitation)

— CHOCOLATE FUDGE SAUCE —

1. Melt chocolate and butter in a sauce pan.
2. Mix in sugar and cream, alternately. Bring to a boil, stirring constantly.
3. Boil and stir 8 minutes, or until thick and creamy.
4. Add vanilla and cool. Yield: about 1 quart.

— PIE —

5. With a spoon, spread 1/2 of ice cream on crust, sprinkle 1/2 pecan pieces on ice cream. Pour 1/2 sauce over pecans.
6. Repeat with second 1/2 of ice cream, pecan and sauce. Place in freezer until ready to serve.
7. To serve, cut in portions while frozen. Top with whipped cream and pecan pieces.

Serves: 9
Preparation: 15 minutes

"Irresistible!"

Villa Nova

D'Agostino/Rodriguez

Almost in the center of the state, near Orlando, is a wonderful family owned restaurant, Villa Nova, that is the center of attention in this popular city. From the first glance, the Roman style arched portico and red tile roof suggest a graceful old villa. Interior accents of brown and soft rose blend with the rich walnut wood and shadowbox moldings on the walls to give the aura of a private club. A large portrait of a smiling Joseph and Antonetta D'Agostino welcomes guests in the foyer.

It was in 1948 that Joseph and Antonetta, who later became affectionately known as Mama and Papa Joe, decided to open a restaurant. To them it became a Villa Nova — "a new home". It was, and still is, home to their children and grandchildren. Where once Papa Joe greeted guests, now his grandsons Mark or John Rodriguez make everyone welcome. No detail is too small to escape the watchful eye of Mama and Papa Joe's daughter Jeanne, who is to her staff like the maestro to his orchestra.

Everyone enjoys the convival atmosphere and that extra little touch of care and concern. Diners can select continental favorites such as *Veal Oscar* or *Chateaubriand*, or American classics such as *New York Strip Sirloin*. Italian favorites include *Linguine with Lobster Sauce Napolitana*, or *Fettucine Alfredo. Escargot and Shrimp Medici* is a truly regal appetizer

— and it isn't necessary to be as rich as the Medici's to enjoy it! The Rodriguez family is constantly updating the menu and creating new ways to please their guests. Often, they name a culinary creation after a patron who suggested what he would like and challenged Mark to make it. *Lobster Russell K* and *Scampi Devaul* are two examples of Villa Nova originals.

Villa Nova is a restaurant with a award winning history. They've been winning Florida Trend Magazine's Golden Spoon Award since 1966. The D'Agostino/Rodriguez family has a tradition of fine food and service for three generations — certainly that's a tradition worth maintaining. . . and a tradition worth your visit.

Take I-4 east in Orlando to Winter Park. Exit on Lee Road. Go south on Lee Road to the end, then north on 17-92 for one block. Villa Nova is at 839 N. Orlando Avenue.

Reservations Suggested.

SCAMPI DEVAUL

12	large raw shrimp - deveined and butterflied
2	T. butter
1	oz. cognac
	grated rind of 1 orange
	juice of 1 orange
1	T. sugar
1	T. Madras curry powder

1. Sauté shrimp in butter. Add cognac and carefully ignite.
2. Add rind and reduce* sauce.
3. Mix orange juice, sugar and curry powder in a glass, and pour over shrimp. Cook until sauce reduces and shrimp are done. Do not overcook.

*See Glossary
Serves: 2
Preparation: 10 minutes
Cooking: 10 minutes

"A curried-citrus flavor makes this an interesting appetizer or main course!"

— NOTES —

LOBSTER RUSSELL K

1   medium sized lobster tail
2   T. butter
2-3 scallions (chopped)
1½ oz. dry white wine
6   oz. heavy whipping cream

1. Remove lobster from shell and sauté in butter until done.
2. Add scallions and white wine. Cook until wine is reduced.
3. Add cream and cook until cream bubbles. Divide between two individual serving plates.

Serves: 2
Preparation: 5 minutes
Cooking: 15-20 minutes

"An appetizer of delicate but subtle flavor!"

— NOTES —

TOURNEDOS KING JACQUES

2   4 oz. beef fillets
8   oz. king crab legs (may use frozen, thaw and drain well)
4   oz. clarified butter*
4   oz. brown sauce* (See Glossary or may purchase)
1   oz. heavy cream
1   oz. cognac
     fresh ground black pepper
2-3   oz. sliced pepper almonds
1   oz. Cream de Noyaux
     bouquetiere of vegetables (*See Note)

1.   In separate pans, sauté the fillets and sauté the crab legs in butter.
2.   To the fillets add cognac, flame carefully and reduce sauce. Add brown sauce and cream. Cook until bubbly and season with pepper.
3.   To the crab legs add almonds, and simmer 1 minute. Add cream de noyaux and flame carefully.
4.   To serve, place the fillets and crab legs on the same warmed plate separated by a bouquetiere* of vegetables.

*NOTE: A combination of vegetables such as green bean and peas, cauliflowerettes and tiny glazed carrots, or artichoke hearts and peas.

*See Glossary
Serves: 2
Preparation: 10 minutes
Cooking: 10-14 minutes

"An intriguing taste combination."

VINTON'S
French - New Orleans Cuisine

It was *worth* spending a sleepy, sultry afternoon in downtown Lake Wales one Saturday just to discover Vinton's. Vinton's, properly known as Vinton's New Orleans, is named for its chef-owner-founder Vinton Davis, who has since turned over operations to his capable and lovely wife Nettie. She is ably assisted by Chefs Edward and James, and the Davis children, Nancy and Joey.

Vinton's New Orleans is located in the Rhodesbilt Arcade built in 1924, which is in itself a treat for lovers of the Roaring 20's eclectic decor. Black and white tile floors, brick courtyards, hanging greenery, dark woods, and stained glass contribute to the mall's charming personality. Vinton's echoes this ambiance with loads of jazzy red razzmatazz! Bright red tablecloths covered by delicate white lace and plush red wall coverings, and the glow of antique leaded glass, lend warmth to the dining room and an intriguing contrast to the freshness of the lush greenery.

Nettie is there to greet you with a smile and a fresh flower as she escorts you to your table. Courteous waitresses, dressed as demure French maids, bring pillows for the ladies' feet, Champagne Cocktails, and fresh fruit salads of Pineapple, Melons, and Triple Sec served in graceful swans. Nettie explains that the pineapple is a symbol of hospitality, as she wants all her guests to feel welcome.

Unique dishes such as *Filet Mignon with Blackberry Sauce* appear on the carefully lettered blackboard menus, along with traditional New Orleans dishes like *Shrimp Bisque. Crablegs Florentine,* and *Roast Crisp Duckling L'Orange Flambe'* making a guest feel not only welcome at Vinton's but absolutely cherished! Top off that perfect dinner with a scandalously rich dessert like *Chocolate Mousse,* and it's easy to see why Vinton's New Orleans is not only chic, but MAGNIFIQUE!

At the intersection of U.S.60 and Alternate 27, proceed north into Lake Wales up to Park Avenue, then west onto Park (Park is a one-way street and the only way to go is west). It's approximately half a block to the Rhodesbilt Arcade and Vinton's.

Reservations Suggested.

VINTON'S SHRIMP BISQUE

1	lb. raw shrimp
1	cup water (or enough to cover shrimp)
3	chicken bouillon cubes
1	T. paprika
½	cup dry sherry
3	T. butter
1	T. flour
1	qt. milk
	salt and pepper to taste

1. Cook shrimp in boiling water 2 minutes, save liquid. Shell and devein shrimp.
2. Add bouillon cubes, paprika and sherry to liquid and boil 2 minutes.
3. In another pan, melt butter, blend in flour and stir in the boiled liquid, cooking until thickened.
4. Slowly stir in milk and simmer. Add shrimp, salt and pepper. Reheat if necessary and serve.

Serves: 4
Preparation: 5 minutes
Cooking: 20 minutes

"A distinctive taste—very good! Be sure to use a good fresh paprika."

— NOTES —

ROAST CRISP DUCKLING L'ORANGE

1　4-5 lb. duck (no heavier—they become tough as they gain weight)
　　salt, pepper
　　oregano
½　orange

— ORANGE-APRICOT SAUCE —

1　6-oz. can frozen orange concentrate
1　cup apricots with juice (canned, peeled and pitted)
¼　cup dark brown sugar
2　T. lemon juice
1　T. triple sec
1　T. brandy

1. Sprinkle duck all over with salt, pepper and oregano. Insert orange half in the cavity.
2. Roast at 350° for 2 hours or until tender. Cool, wrap in foil and refrigerate until next day.
4. Roast the duck ½ hour more before serving, basting continually with orange sauce.

— ORANGE-APRICOT SAUCE —

3. Mix sauce ingredients in blender or food processor. Yield 2 cups.

Serves: 2
Preparation: 5/5 minutes
Cooking: 2½ hours

"Works perfectly—and is simply divine!"

CHOCOLATE MOUSSE

1   6-oz. pkg. semi-sweet chocolate bits
6   egg yolks (beaten)
1   t. vanilla
6   egg whites (stiffly beaten)

1. Melt chocolate bits in double boiler.
2. Carefully blend in egg yolks, making sure chocolate is not so hot that it curdles the eggs.
3. Stir in vanilla.
4. Remove from heat and fold in stiffly-beaten egg whites.
5. Pour in individual serving dishes and refrigerate.

Serves: 4-6
Preparation: 10 minutes
Cooking: 8 minutes

"An easy classic!"

— NOTES —

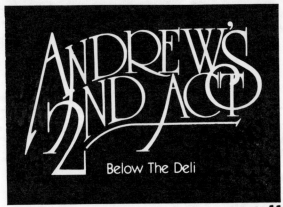

Below The Deli

This restaurant purports to carry the distinction of being the first gourmet house in Tallahassee.

Don't be surprised if you happen to run into the Senate majority leader, as this is one of the favorite dining establishments of Florida politicians. Its proximity to the Capitol makes for an interesting composite of clientele.

Andrew Reiss, a young entrepreneur and graduate of the Restaurant School at Florida State has managed to create four different operations under one main complex: Maxin's Seafood Bar and Lounge, The Brass Rail, Tutto Béné with its fine northern Italian cuisine, and our favorite, Andrew's 2nd Act. There was no doubt in my mind the the 2nd Act deserves a standing ovation for excellence in continental cuisine.

The decor is casual, yet 'ritzy,' with its quaint European flavor blending favorably with the sumptuous cuisine. Andrew's daily specials are popular with local patrons. Each day a different beef, foul, veal and seafood dinner is featured. Their uniqueness is undoubtably why this restaurant has been the recipient of the Florida Trend Magazine Golden Spoon Award for the past four years.

We suggest the *Mozzarella Marinara* as a truly unique appetizer. Mozzarella cheese balls are deep fried and topped with a delectable creole sauce. For dessert, try the *Creme Brulee*, heavenly baked custard crowned with a luscious fruit flambé—or, feast on one of Andrew's famous dessert crepes.

Enjoy the capitol city at a capital restaurant. Andrew's 2nd Act is "1st class" in our book.

To find Andrew's in downtown Tallahassee, head one block north of the Capitol on Adams Street Mall. Andrews is located on the corner of Adams and Jefferson streets.

Reservations Suggested.

CHICKEN SUNRISE

8	chicken breasts (skinned and boned)
2	sticks butter (8 ounces)

— MUSTARD SAUCE —

½	cup prepared mustard
1	cup dry white wine

— FRANCAISE BATTER —

5	eggs
½	pint heavy cream
½	cup freshly grated Parmesan
¼	cup parsley (chopped)

— TOPPING —

2	avocados (peeled, cut into 16 slices)
8	oz. Alaskan king crab chunks
4	oz. Gruyère cheese (8 slices)

— MUSTARD SAUCE —

1. Mix mustard and wine together.

— FRANCAISE BATTER—

2. Beat together with a wire whisk the eggs, cream, parmesan and parsley.

— TO PREPARE CHICKEN —

3. Dip chicken in mustard sauce, then in Francaise batter.
4. Sauté in butter (approx. 2T. per breast) until tender. Crust should be golden brown and thick.

-continued-

5. Top each breast with 2 avocado slices, 1 oz. king crab and 1 slice (½ oz.) Gruyére cheese. Run under broiler until cheese melts.

Serves: 8
Preparation: 20 minutes
Cooking: 30-35 minutes

"A special way to prepare chicken for your next dinner party."

– NOTES –

TOURNEDOS ST. LAURENT

6	**8-oz. filet mignons**
½	**clove fresh garlic (chopped)**
6	**green onions (chopped)**
¼	**cup fresh parsley (chopped—no stems)**
½	**lb. butter (clarified*)**
18	**spears fresh asparagus (steamed)**

1. Sauté garlic, green onions and parsley in 3 T. butter. When mixture begins to brown add remaining butter and blend. Keep warm.
2. Charbroil filets to order. Make 3 1-inch cuts on top of each steak to form a pocket.
3. Place an asparagus spear in each pocket. Top each steak with 1/4 of sauce. Serve immediately.

*See Glossary
Serves: 6
Preparation: 15 minutes
Cooking: 10/10 minutes

"An appealing presentation."

— NOTES —

CRÈME BRÛLÉE
(Allow overnight to chill)

1   quart heavy whipping cream
½   cup sugar
8   egg yolks
1   T. vanilla
     brown sugar (enough to cover top of custard
     completely)

— TOPPING —
fruit with juice (such as strawberries or cherries)

1. In a double boiler warm cream and sugar (do not boil) until sugar dissolves.
2. Beat eggs until fluffy. Beat into cream mixture with a wire whisk. Add vanilla. Heat until mixture thickens, stirring constantly.
3. Pour into individual dishes and set in 1 inch of water in a shallow baking pan. Bake in a slow oven at 275° for 1 hour or until set.
4. Remove from oven. Cool. Refrigerate over night.
5. To serve, sprinkle brown sugar on top and lightly pack. Place under broiler just long enough to caramelize sugar.
6. Top with fruit.

Serves: 8
Preparation: 10 minutes
Cooking: 15/1 hour
Chill: Overnight
Broil: Until caramelized

"Because most of the recipe is made the day before, it's the ideal dessert to serve for parties. Everyone loves it."

BROTHERS THREE
Restaurant

tallahassee

Since the ripe young age of 14 years, Jimmy Koikos can remember the tantalizing aromas surfacing from his mother's "Spartan" kitchen. And now Jimmy, along with brothers George and Pete bring a touch of Greece to the patrons of the popular Brothers Three restaurant in Tallahassee.

The three siblings have skillfully managed to create the best in quality steaks and seafood dishes. Nine beautifully decorated rooms create intimate dining alcoves in the cheeriest of English country settings.

Begin a pleasurable evening with the *Fresh Appalachicola Oysters* or the *Golden Brown Crab Claws*. The Brothers' Prime Steaks are done to perfection; the seafood platters are among the most bountiful in the sunshine state. Along with each entrée is included the Brothers' famous salad bar with large chunks of Feta cheese and mounds of imported Greek olives.

The Brothers Three, with their cordial conviviality "put it all together" with excellent beef and fish entrées.

Be sure to enjoy a truly memorable meal in northern Florida and enjoyable Tallahassee.

To arrive at the Brothers Three Restaurant, take U.S. 27 north and Exit I-10 to 2696 North Monroe.

BAKED OYSTERS APPALACHICOLA

— FOR 1 SERVING —

6	oysters (well cleaned, drained and returned to shell)
6	drops Worcestershire sauce
6	drops Tabasco
	salt and pepper to taste
1	slice bacon (cut 6 pieces partially cooked)
6	T. chili sauce
3	t. Parmesan cheese

1. On each oyster, add 1 drop Worcestershire, 1 drop Tabasco, salt and pepper.
2. Top with bacon piece, 1 T. chili sauce, ½ t. Parmesan.
3. Bake in preheated oven 350°-400° for 10 minutes.

Serves: 1
Preparation: 10 minutes
Cooking: 10 minutes

"Quick and easy appetizer!"

— NOTES —

ROAST LEG OF LAMB

1	5 lb. leg of lamb
4	cloves garlic (sliced)
½	cup rose wine
	juice of 2 lemons
1	t. oregano
	salt and pepper to taste

1. Score leg of lamb as you would a ham. Make slits in each diamond shape and insert garlic slices until used.
2. Pour wine and lemon juice over. Sprinkle with oregano, salt and pepper.
3. Bake 375° for 1½ hours—longer if you prefer it very well done. Serve with potato wedges, rolled in oil and baked with lamb. Run potatoes under broiler to brown. Salt and pepper. Sprinkle with parsley.

Serves: 6
Preparation: 10 minutes
Cooking: 1½ hours

"For variety, you may rub in extra herbs to your taste, such as ginger, bay, thyme, marjoram and soy."

— NOTES —

Capt. Anderson's
RESTAURANT
ON GRAND LAGOON

panama city

The residents will tell you—without ever being asked—that Capt. Anderson's is not only their pride and joy, but also one of America's top seafood restaurants. And that's not difficult to believe after glancing over the daily logs which record upwards of 2000 diners daily during peak periods.

A large, yet intimate facility, the Anderson covers over 26,000 square feet of space and boasts nearly 150 dedicated employees. Most impressive is the eagerness of the beaming staff. Perhaps this is due to the two-month gratus vacation the owners allow when the restaurant closes its doors each year from November through January 1.

Once inside, it's obvious that Johnny and Jimmy Patronis, owners since 1967 have discovered the secret ingredient for maintaining consistently superior quality and service.

Situated dockside on the Grand Lagoon near scenic highway 98 and adjacent to "The World's Most Beautiful Beaches" proudly stands the Capt. Anderson Restaurant. Well worth rearranging your itinerary to accommodate, the restaurant offers a dramatic panoramic view of a fleet of fishing vessels anchored only a few yards away. The three spacious dining rooms and accompanying lounge are tastefully decorated by the two Greek brothers in rustic nautical motif with the rarest of marine artifacts.

The menu has a wide selection of entrées that were most extraordinary. I decided on the fresh caught *Red Snapper* grilled whole over a blazing charcoal fire. Its special Grecian-style sauce was most pleasing. Johnny explained how the recipe has been in his family for nearly centuries.

Other mouth watering entrées include the *Grilled Bay Shrimp,* the *Fried Tenderloin of Grouper* and the Captain's "favorite," *Stuffed Jumbo Gulf Shrimp.*

One of the most exciting salads I've ever tried was the Anderson's *Tomato Greek Salad* laden with Feta cheese, greek olives and Salonika peppers. The famous hard rolls from the on-premise bakery were some of the best ever sampled. Try the *Baklava* and top off the meal with a bottle of White Domestica—and you have an evening in Athens, a la Florida!

And by all means, don't forget to introduce yourself to the Patronis brothers. They won't forget you!

Pierside on the Grand Lagoon, Panama City.

TOMATO GREEK SALAD WITH
CRABMEAT AND SHRIMP
(Seafood salad from the Greek Islands)

— DRESSING —

2	T. Lawry's seasoned salt
1	T. oregano
1	T. black pepper
2	cloves garlic (crushed)
1½	cups olive oil
1½	cups salad oil
¼	cup red wine vinegar
¼	cup water

— FOR EACH SERVING —

1	tomato (quartered)
6	cucumber slices
4	mild Greek peppers (Salonika or Pepperocini)
6	colossal Calamata olives
2	oz. Feta cheese
4-6	shrimp (boiled and peeled)
2	oz. lump crabmeat (flaked)
2	slices avocado
2	anchovy strips
4	slices red onion

— DRESSING —

1. Combine all ingredients. Shake very well before each use. Yield: 1 quart.

— SALAD —

2. Arrange ingredients on a lettuce leaf with crab in center. Top with avocado and anchovies. Garnish with red onion. Pour dressing over all.

Preparation: 15 minutes

"This very light dressing is enhancing, even for other salads!"

GRECIAN-STYLE CHARCOAL BROILED
SILVER POMPANO

— FOR EACH SERVING —

1½	lb. whole Pompano (cleaned and sealed)
2	T. olive oil
3	T. scallions (chopped)
3	T. parsley (chopped)
	salt and pepper to taste

— SAUCE —

2/3	cup butter
1/3	cup olive oil
¼	cup lemon juice

1. Rub oil over fish and charcoal 7 minutes on each side. Do not overcook. (An oiled fish rack is handy—2 cake racks tied together with wire will work nicely.)
2. Blend sauce ingredients over heat. Place fish on a platter. Pour sauce over it. (Fish should swim in sauce.) Salt and pepper. Sprinkle with scallions and parsley.

Serves: 1
Preparation: 10 minutes
Cooking: 14 minutes

"Unbelievably good. Will work well for other similar fish!"

— NOTES —

FEUD CAKE

6	eggs (separated)
1½	cups sugar
2½	T. flour
1	t. baking powder (sifted)
3	cups finely ground pecans (2 6½-oz. packages)
1	pint whipped cream, flavored with vanilla and 2 T. sugar

1. Beat egg yolks until fluffy. Gradually add sugar, beating constantly.
2. Add flour and baking power.
3. Add ground pecans and fold in stiffly-beaten egg whites.
4. Bake in 2 layer pans for 30 minutes at 350°.
5. To serve, ice with whipped cream between layers, top and sides. Sprinkle with ground pecans.

Serves: 8
Preparation: 15 minutes
Cooking: 30 minutes

"This was named "Feud" cake because of the age-long family feud, as to who originated this delicious recipe. It is out of this world!"

— NOTES —

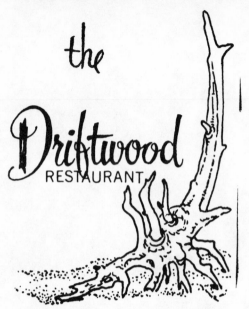

the Driftwood RESTAURANT

pensacola

Since 1953, The Driftwood has been *the* location in the five-flag city of Pensacola for "exciting" cuisine.

Founded over a quarter of a century ago, George Banakas developed this quiet retreat, just recently turning the operation over to a most capable daughter, Stephanie Carnley and son-in-law, William Terrell Carnley.

A family operated gourmet restaurant, the continental cuisine has elicited fond proclamations from patrons throughout the state. Exquisite paintings by Mr. Banakas grace the delicate scenery with its magnificent 25 foot ceilings and elegant decor. Fresh pink carnations, with tender baby's breath in white porcelain vases enhance the precious royal blue and white china. A true pastel palette aesthetically combined in a most exquisite manner!

Holiday season at The Driftwood magically recreates a winter wonderland in this northernmost Florida city.

Enjoy the seafood casseroles, the famous *She-Crab Stew*, the tantalizing breads and desserts and the fresh seafood. Among the local favorites are the *Filet of Flounder Mornay* and the *Casserole of Artichoke Hearts with Fresh Lump Crab au Gratin*. The unparalleled ecstacy of these dishes in guaranteed by the consistency of the husband-wife team of chefs.

The Driftwood is truly worth the travel time!

To locate the Driftwood Restaurant, take Exit 110 off the Interstate at 27 W. Garden Street, Pensacola. Keep your eyes open!

Reservations Suggested.

SHE-CRAB STEW

1	lb. she-crab meat (crab with roe)
	or lump crab meat (well picked over)
½	onion chopped
1/3	cup butter
1/3	cup flour
1	cup half and half
2	qts. whole milk
1½	T. Worcestershire sauce
1	T. salt
	white pepper to taste
1/3	cup dry sherry

1. Sauté onions in butter. Add flour and mix well.
2. Slowly add cream and milk, stirring constantly.
3. Add Worcestershire sauce, salt and crabmeat. Heat through.
4. Add white pepper and sherry. Serve hot.

Serves: 8-10
Preparation: 5 minutes
Cook: 10 minutes

"This is a lovely soup course with a decidedly different flavor, especially with she-crab meat!"

— NOTES —

ASPARAGUS SALAD MOLD
(Allow time to chill)

3	10 oz. cans asparagus
	water
3	pkg. (3 T.) Knox gelatin
3	T. water
1	cup mayonnaise
¼	cup lemon juice
4	oz. whipped cream
	salt and white pepper to taste
½	cup slivered almonds

1. Drain asparagus, reserving juice. Cut in thirds.
2. In a sauce pan, add enough water to juice to make 2 cups and heat. Add gelatin, which has been dissolved in 3 T. water to juice and blend well.
3. Remove from heat. Stir in mayonnaise, lemon juice, whipped cream, salt and pepper.
4. When partially set, fold in asparagus and almonds. Pour in 6 cup oiled mold and chill until firm.

Serves: 8
Preparation: 30 minutes
Chill: 2-3 hours

"Easy to prepare and so refreshing."

— NOTES —

TELEPHONE

POLICE

CARRABELLE, FLA.

Police Station, Carrabelle Florida

JULIA MAE'S TOWN-INN

INC

carrabelle

Carrabelle, a miniature town in Franklin County, on the edge of Appalachicola County is well known for two reasons. One is for housing the smallest police station in the United States (which incidentally, operates within the confines of a telephone booth). And the other is Julia Mae Putnal, owner, manager and chief cook at Julia Mae's famous Town Inn.

Julia Mae has created enjoyable seafood feasts for well over thirty years and is nearly a legend to the townfolk. Her "angler" husband contributes the fresh sea catch while sisters Audrey and Merle serve scores of anxious customers. Hearty entrées include the freshest of snapper, mullet, grouper, fresh water catfish, and as one regular said, "The sweetest oysters ever had!"

Julia Mea's *Seafood Gumbo, Deviled Crab* and "melt-in-mouth" *Hushpuppies* bring forth such guest-register comments as "The best seafood in the world, also the most!" Her luscious variety of creme pies (fresh out of her "pie house"), together with such favorites as her mountainous bowl of banana pudding (created only on Sundays) are known to cause such remarks as "It sure was great, Julia Mae, I'll be back Appalachicola!"

Set back from the main roadway among stately pines, the scene is primitive, yet romantic. Upon entering the barn-like structure, your eyes focus on a cartooned picture of an out-house which explains "The restrooms are outside."

Just inside, one notices a neatly framed letter which reads, "It was a pleasure visiting Julia Mae's during our trip to the Seafood Festival. We had heard much about your restaurant and it certainly surpasses its reputation." Signed, the Governor of Florida.

Dress is very casual—there are no frills in this decor. Walls are flanked with a potpourri of varied sea paraphernalia and local memorabilia. Julia Mae's Town Inn is certainly not for the finicky gourmet or fancy diner, but for the connoisseur of delectable seafood and "fixins."

Julia Mae's is located on U.S. 98, approximately 50 miles south of Tallahassee, in Carrabelle.

No need to worry about Reservations!

JULIA MAE'S FAMOUS COCONUT PIE

2	cups milk
4	T. butter
3	eggs (separated)
2½	T. cornstarch
½	cup sugar
1	t. vanilla
4	oz. coconut
1	9" pie crust (baked)
2	T. sugar

1. In top of a double boiler, heat milk and butter until very hot.
2. Stirring constantly, add egg yolks slowly. Beat in cornstarch, sugar and vanilla.
3. When thickened, add coconut, reserving enough to toast on top of pie. Pour into crust.
4. Beat egg whites for meringue, adding 2 T. of sugar. Spread on top of pie and sprinkle with remaining coconut. Heat in 400° oven for 5-8 minutes, or until nicely browned.

Serves: 8
Preparation: 15 minutes
Cooking: 15 minutes

"Simply melts in your mouth!"

— NOTES —

Capt. Jim's
CONCH HUT
st. augustine

About seven great grandfathers ago, James Augustine Ponce's ancestor helped build the Castillo de San Marcos. About twenty years ago, Ponce and his energetic sons, Dave and Jim began collecting materials to build the Conch House.

The Conch House is a close replica of the Capo Bath House built in 1870, burned in 1914, and once located off the seawall slightly north of the famous Bridge of Lions. Masterfully designed and decorated in nautical overtones, and actually located over the water, it is truly a mariner's museum. A brass gimbled compass located in the center of the House and a solid bronze windlass once used to raise anchors are just a sampling of this magnificent family project.

Just adjacent to the Conch House and allowing for a perfect view of the waterway, the Ponce family built Capt. Jim's Conch Hut, a cozy informal eating house. Local residents recommend the Hut for excellent *Minorcan Conch Chowder.* After a hearty sampling of the famous family recipe, generously offered by son Dave, there was little doubt that the locals were accurate in their advice! The huge chunks of Bahamian Conch were delectable.

Ponce, a merry yarn spinner well known around town as one of the "last of the true blooded Minorcans" has been said to have as much brass content as the ship's bell that hangs over the bar. His outrageous stories are a fitting appetizer to his fresh seafood dinners. A warm and most hospitable family, the Ponces are typical of the casual Florida lifestyle.

Top off your visit with one of Capt. Jim's oversized fruity concoctions such as the fresh *Honeydew Daiquiri* laden with great slabs of melon and strawberries. Let the Conch Hut entertain you—you can count on a "real good time."

Arrive by land or sea — By Land: across the Bridge of Lions, A1A South, six blocks; turn left at the sign, two and a half blocks to "By The Sea," 57 Comares Avenue, St. Augustine. By Sea: follow markers to "By The Sea" Marina, just south of St. Augustine Inlet in Salt Run.

No Reservations Necessary!

CONCH CHOWDER
(Made from an old Minorcan family recipe)

12	oz. conch meat or clams (well cleaned)
1/8	lb. salt pork (chopped fine)
2	onions (chopped fine)
1	bell pepper (chopped fine)
1-2	datil* peppers (or hottest pepper for substitute)
3	cups canned tomatoes (chopped)
2	cups canned potatoes (diced)
½	cup tomato puree
½	T. thyme
½	T. salt
½	T. fresh ground pepper
1-2	bay leaves (crushed)

1. Sauté pork in large pot. Remove and set aside.
2. Add onions, bell peppers and sauté. Add hot peppers.
3. Add reserved pork and remaining ingredients.
4. Bring to boil 15 minutes. Simmer 45 minutes to 1 hour.

Serves: 6-8
Preparation: 15 minutes
Cooking: 1 hour

"Wonderful robust flavor!!"

*Datil peppers are very hot and may be difficult to find. The Ponce family has them "custom" grown for their seafood dishes. If you can't find your own datil peppers write David Ponce and he'll send you the name of a supplier.

SEA FOOD GUMBO

1/8	lb. salt pork (diced)
½	cup onion (diced)
1	cup fresh okra (sliced)
2	10 oz. cans tomatoes w/juice (diced)
1	t. thyme
1½	t. fresh ground black pepper
1	lb. raw shrimp (cut in pieces)
¼	datil pepper*
	salt to taste

1. Fry pork until brown. Remove from pan and reserve.
2. Add onions to grease. Sauté until clear. Add okra. Stir 10 minutes.
3. Add remaining ingredients and pork. Simmer 20-30 minutes.
4. Serve over rice. Garnish with lemon wedges and parsley.

Serves: 4-6
Preparation: 20 minutes
Cooking: 30-40 minutes

*NOTE: Datil peppers are *very* hot. If you have difficulty finding Datil peppers, you may substitute the hottest peppers you can find. Taste gumbo before adding too much.

"The spicy-hot seasoning is what makes Capt. Jim's famous for his gumbo!!"

— NOTES —

THE CHART HOUSE

st. augustine

Twenty-five years before the United States was born, The Old Spanish House in St. Augustine was first built. Located on the picturesque Avenida Menéndez, this ancient structure is the site of The Chart House Restaurant.

The foundations of the house, arch and gate date back to the 1700's. Its graceful coquina shell archway welcomes all nationalities to our country's oldest city founded by Pedro Menéndez De Avilés in 1565.

The decor is nautical with deeply hued ocean "charts" beautifully embedded in handsome wooden tables. Valuable antiques displayed throughout the house, make one envision Ponce De Leon himself enjoying a feast here after his discovery of "La Florida" (meaning "flowered") on Easter Sunday in 1513.

A Florida Trend Golden Spoon Award winner, this time-honored restaurant's wooden menu boards boast healthy portions of prime rib, the freshest of seafood from nearby waters, hot homestyle bread (all you can eat) and the one and only Chart House "mud pie" for dessert!

A refreshing, and financially pleasing touch is The Chart House's amiable outlook on family dining. A special 'kid's menu' features smaller portions of the adult menu with "tot-size" prices. Children receive complimentary soft drinks and a Chart House balloon. And, to keep them quiet while you enjoy the scenery, the clever take-home menu has a treasure hunt puzzle, a coloring page and a 'connect the dot' parrot. The Chart House knows nothing makes a parent happier than a happy child!

Enjoy The Chart House as part of the history of St. Augustine, and part of Florida's heritage of excellent cuisine.

Chart your way to The Chart House located at 46 Avenue Menéndez, 40 yards from the Bridge of Lions in downtown St. Augustine.

CHART HOUSE THOUSAND ISLAND DRESSING

1	pt. whole egg mayonnaise
½	cup catsup
¼	red onion (minced)
1	stalk celery (minced)
1	sweet pickle (minced)
¼	green pepper (minced)
1	sprig parsley (minced)
1	T. pimiento (minced)
1	egg (hard cooked and chopped)
	salt and pepper to taste

1. Mix the mayonnaise and catsup thoroughly.
2. Blend in the remaining ingredients and refrigerate until ready to serve.

Yield: About 2½-3 cups

"Perfection"

— NOTES —

CHARTHOUSE BLEU CHEESE DRESSING
(allow 24 hours for refrigeration)

¾	cup sour cream
½	t. dry mustard
½	t. black pepper
½	t. salt (scant)
1/3	t. garlic powder (scant)
1	t. Worcestershire sauce
1-1/3	cups mayonnaise
4	oz. imported Danish bleu cheese (aged)

1. In a mixer bowl, blend sour cream, mustard, pepper, salt, garlic powder and Worcestershire for 2 minutes at low speed.
2. Add mayonnaise. Blend 1/2 minute at low speed and 2 minutes at medium speed.
3. By hand, crumble cheese into mixture. Blend at low speed no more than 4 minutes. Refrigerate.

Yield: 2½ cups
Chill: 24 hours

"One of the best!!"

— NOTES —

CHART HOUSE MUD PIE
(Allow time to freeze)

½	package Nabisco Chocolate Wafers*
½	stick butter melted
1½	quarts coffee ice cream (softened)
1½	cups fudge sauce (see Chalet Suzanne, Sauce w/Gateau Christina on page 215.)
1	pint whipping cream (whipped)
½	cup almonds (toasted)

1. Crush wafers, add butter, mix well and press into 9" pie plate. Chill about 15 minutes.
2. Mound softened ice cream in crust making sure center is high and lush looking. Place in freezer until firm.
3. Make fudge sauce (your own or the excellent one suggested). Refrigerate to achieve spreading consistency. Spread over ice cream—freeze until ready to serve.
4. Cut into wedges. Serve with a dollop of whipped cream topped with toasted almonds.

Serves: 8
Preparation: 25 minutes
Freeze: 2-3 hours

*In the event Nabisco Chocolate Wafers are hard to find, just use Nabisco Oreos (about 20 double cookies). Scrape out the filling and give it to a child who does this as a matter of course. Proceed as above.

"A Chart House favorite!"

— NOTES —

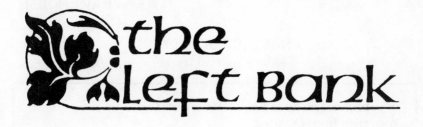

the Left Bank

After a tedious drive across nearly half the width of Northern Florida to this far Northeast corner, Jacksonville was a pleasing sight. And even more enjoyable was my genial welcome at this intimate European style oasis.

A 1981 Florida Trend Golden Spoon Award winner, The Left Bank, in a short span of two years, has been noted by many to be the best restaurant in the city, excelling in fine European cuisine and service.

Certified Executive Chef Wilfried Hausy together with Owner Paul McLaughlin present a most inviting menu along with a most convivial atmosphere. Carnation-decked tables add a touch of romance and intrigue.

Try the *Champignons Farcis*, beef-stuffed select mushrooms in sour cream sauce- a most delectable appetizer! Chef Wilfred insisted I eat his famous *Caesar Salad* with my fingers, to insure the freshness of the large green leaves. He was right! Caesar himself would have devoured this one.

The owner's specialty, appropriately named, *Paul's Favorite* was a fresh grouper filet wrapped in romaine and baked in luscious light pastry with a delightful *Sauce Choron*. A perfect complement is the tantalizing *Strawberries Romanoff*. A meal fit for a king. . .and that is also how you are treated.

The Left Bank, which incidentally is not on the left bank at all (which goes to prove that all good restaurants are not on the left bank!), is certainly earning its reputation for excellence. If you are looking for a perfect evening, you'll find it at The Left Bank.

The Left Bank is located at 1435 University Boulevard North, one-third mile north of Town and Country Shopping Center in Jacksonville.

Reservations Suggested.

CREAM OF WATERCRESS SOUP

2	bundles watercress (washed and stemmed)
2	T. butter
1	T. onions (chopped)
3	T. flour
7	cups chicken stock
½	cup dry white wine
1	chicken bouillon cube
½	cup heavy cream
1	egg yolk (beaten)
	salt to taste
	white pepper to taste
	nutmeg to taste

1. Melt butter. Sauté onions and watercress until onions are transparent.
2. Add flour, stir and remove from heat. Let sit 5 minutes.
3. Heat stock, add to sautéed ingredients. Blend with a wire whisk.
4. Bring mixture to boil, add wine and bouillon cube. Simmer 30 minutes.
5. Strain soup. Purée remaining ingredients in blender. Return to soup. Blend cream with egg yolk using a whisk. Add slowly to soup. Season to taste with salt, pepper and nutmeg.

Serves: 6-8
Preparation: 15 minutes
Cooking: 30 minutes

"A light but elegant soup course!!"
— NOTES —

CELERY ROOT AU GRATIN

2   medium celery roots
2   T. butter (melted)
1   cup celery stock* (See Note)
1   cup Parmesan cheese (grated)

1. Wash roots and boil in salted water until tender, about 35 minutes. When cool, peel and slice in ¼" slices.
2. Place in oven-proof dish. Salt and pepper to taste. Add celery stock. Pour butter over slices. Top with Parmesan.
3. Bake at 350° until cheese is golden brown for about 15-20 minutes.

*NOTE: You may use stock made from boiling celery roots if roots are very thoroughly cleaned. To make your own, simmer chopped celery, with leaves attached, with salt, pepper, and a dash of paprika for one half-hour.

Serves: 6
Preparation: 15 minutes

Cooking/Baking: 35/20 minutes

"A different vegetable—delightful to serve with ham."

— NOTES —

GROUPER A LA LEFT BANK
(Allow 4 hours to marinate)

—FOR EACH SERVING —

6	oz. grouper fillet
½	t. lemon juice
½	t. Worcestershire sauce
	salt and pepper to taste
½	t. thyme
½	t. basil
½	t. majoram
½	t. dry mustard
½	t. curry powder
½	t. coriander
¼	t. ground ginger
2	romaine leaves
6	oz. puff pastry (may be purchased in frozen foods section, Pepperidge Farm brand)
1	clove garlic
1	T. butter
	olive slice (for garnish)
	lemon wedges (for garnish)
	parsley sprigs (for garnish)

1. Marinate fillets in lemon juice mixed with all of the seasonings except garlic and butter for four hours in refrigerator.
2. Poach romaine leaves for 30 seconds. Cool.
3. Roll pastry into thin square.
4. Roll fillet into romaine leaves and place in center of pastry. Spread fish with butter and garlic that have been blended.
5. Fold pastry over fish shaping to resemble a fish. Seal well. Use olive slice for eye. Brush top with milk or beaten egg or milk.
6. Bake at 350° for 20 minutes until pastry is golden brown.
7. Garnish with lemon wedges and parsley sprigs.

-continued-

Serves: 1
Preparation: 15 minutes
Marinate: 4 hours
Bake: 20 minutes

"Guests are delighted with this beautiful entrée. It is not difficult to prepare and is most succulent!"

— NOTES —

Flagler Memorial Presbyterian Church, St. Augustine

Le Guéridon Restaurant

Among St. Augustine's premier restaurants is Le Guéridon, an intimate and popular restaurant specializing in French gourmet cuisine.

Reminiscent of a French country inn, the atmosphere is cozy and romantic. Tantalizing aromas permeate the trio of quaint and friendly dining rooms. Freshly cut flowers, displayed in dainty porcelain vases, suggest a hint of the French countryside.

In addition to the sumptuous selections on the menu, owner chefs Frank Brown and Robert Mark offer several specialité de jour entrées such as *Escargot Mode De L'Abbaye* (snails baked on mushroom caps glazed). Vegetables are prepared in the best French tradition. The *Carrot Gateau—* c'est magnifique!

Delicately baked desserts and pastries displayed in the entry area remind guests to leave a few bites on their plates, if they must, to savor the excellence of true French pastry. Try their tempting *Floating Islands, Apple Tarts* or *Fresh Strawberries in Creme.* A fruit addition to every meal is a French tradition. We insist!

Le Gueridon, in operation for only two years, enjoys a fast growing reputation for the best in culinary delights. Combined with the concerned cordiality of hosts, Frank and Robert, this is one fine restaurant you can't afford to miss!

Though Le Guéridon opened just two years ago, hosts Frank and Robert have mastered the art of dining excellence. Not a single attentive detail is amiss. And their dedication is rewarded with the fastest growing popularity (and regularity of guests) in the area. Discover Le Guéridon's secrets for success.

Le Guéridon Restaurant is located on the north junction of A1A and State Road 3, St. Augustine, on your way to Daytona — easy to find!

Reservations Suggested.

SHRIMP MOUTARDE

20	large raw shrimp (peeled and deveined)
½	cup white wine
½	cup fish stock*
2	T. Dijon mustard
1	t. flour
1	t. butter
¾	cup whipping cream
	salt and pepper to taste
3	T. butter

1. In a sauce pan, heat wine and stock to boiling. Reduce* by ½, stir in mustard.
2. Make a roux* of 1 t. flour and 1 t. butter. Add to sauce stirring constantly. Pour in cream. Salt and pepper to taste.
3. Sauté shrimp in butter. DO NOT overcook. Place in oven-proof dish. Pour sauce over shrimp (may be prepared in advance at this point). Broil until lightly browned.

*See Glossary
Serves: 4
Preparation: 10 minutes
Cooking: 20 minutes

"Placing 5 shrimp in 4 individual ramekins is an attractive way to serve this appetizer!"

— NOTES —

CARROT GATEAU

2½   lbs. carrots (scraped, cut in large slices)
1¼   cups heavy cream
½   cup butter
½   cup water
5   eggs
       salt and white pepper to taste

1. In a saucepan, simmer the carrots with 1/2 cup of the cream, all of the butter and water until tender.
2. Drain liquid from carrots and reduce* it by 3/4. Cool.
3. Beat eggs and remaining 3/4 cup cream, salt and white pepper. Combine with cool liquid from carrots.
4. Pour mixture into carrots. Place all in buttered baking dish, leaving 1/2 " around top, to avoid spillage.
5. Bake at 350° for 1½ hours. Cool slightly to cut in squares.

*See Glossary
Serves: 8
Preparation: 10 minutes
Cooking: 2 hours

"The sweet flavor of carrots prevails in this unusual preparation!"

— NOTES —

EAT, DRINK AND BE MERRIE, THAT'S MY MOTTO

THE SOVEREIGN RESTAURANT

The single element of frustration you will ever experience at The Sovereign, is choosing a dinner entrée from dozens of deliciously described temptations on the menu. Should it be the *Veal Sovereign?* Delicate *Scalloppine of Veal with Mushrooms and Champagne Sauce*, or, the *Chicken Jerusalem* with its masterful mixture of mushrooms, artichokes and fresh scallions? A *Casserole of Drunken Fishes*, the proprietor's creation of shrimp, snapper, scallops, oysters, clams, flounder and lobster beckons a seafood gourmet. But then, so does the *Scallone* with its luscious California Abalone and scallops in a perfectly seasoned sauce.

You could ask Elmo, the Swiss-born owner-chef trained in Pontresina, Switzerland. . .but, he can't decide either! At least you can be assured that regardless of your choice, it was the right one!

A consistent Florida Trend Golden Spoon Award winner, Elmo relates how the Sovereign was once a house of many trades; a warehouse, machine shop, electrical storehouse and even the Carriage House next to "The Opera." Whatever the history, the romantic New Orleans style building with its cathedral ceiling and original brick flooring frequently inspires marriage proposals and special "no occasion" celebrations. Skylights enhance the happy occasion, beaming in the Florida sunshine for you and the myriad of green flowing plants to share.

On Thursdays, Elmo's wife, Lupe, of Mexican descent takes her turn in the kitchen producing Mexican delights of perfection.

Top off a perfectly romantic evening with Elmo's *Chocolate Mousse Cake* or a snifter of *Brandy-Sauced Ice Cream!* Take Elmo seriously when he says "I promise you the best food in Gainesville."

Off I-75, east on 26 to Main Street, two blocks south of Main Street at 12 Second Avenue.   *Reservations Suggested.*

CHICKEN JERUSALEM

4	chicken breasts (skinned and boned)
	salt and pepper
	flour
½	cup frying oil
1	T. butter
½	cup fresh chives or green onions (chopped fine)
1	cup mushrooms (sliced)
8	oz. sour cream (room temperature)
1	can artichoke hearts

1. Salt and pepper chicken. Roll lightly in flour, sauté in oil until just done. Remove from pan and keep warm.
2. Drain oil from pan. Add 1 T. butter, sauté onions and mushrooms until tender. Remove from heat and stir in sour cream. Heat again. (If sauce seems too thick, add a little white wine.)
3. Place heated artichoke hearts on warm chicken. Dress with sauce.

Serves: 4
Preparation: 10 minutes
Cooking: 15 minutes

"An enticing offering. All ingredients go splendidly with the chicken."

— NOTES —

LOMO SALTADO A LA GRIOLLA
(Beef with Peppers)

24	oz. beef tenderloin strips (1" long, ½" thick)
1	large onion (sliced)
1	red pepper (sliced)
1	green pepper (sliced)
2	cloves garlic (chopped fine)
3	oz. pimentos (sliced)
8	dashes of Tabasco
	salt and pepper to taste
1	cup demi-glace or brown sauce*
	rice

1. Sauté onions, peppers in small amount of oil. Add garlic and shake pan.
2. Add beef and sauté until rare. Add pimentos, spices and demi-glace. Mix well and serve over rice.

*See Glossary
Serves: 4
Preparation: 5 minutes
Cook: 10 minutes

"Make this as spicy as you like. Very attractive to serve."

— NOTES —

— NOTES —

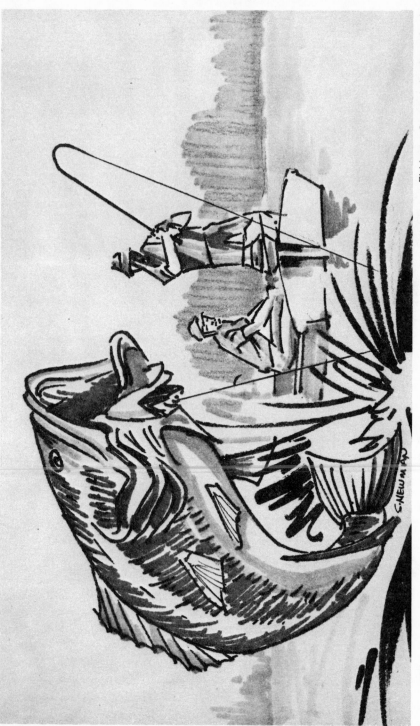

THE YEARLING RESTAURANT

cross creek

Just south of the bridge that spans the sleepy village of Cross Creek near Gainesville, and next to the home of Pulitzer-prize winning author Marjorie Kinnan Rawlings, stands a rustic, red-barn restaurant and inn named after the author's most famous novel. The Yearling, nestled near a creek between two large bass lakes, holds a special appeal for the "outdoorsman" in everyone. Resident owners Herb and Pat Herman, with their warm hearts and kind hospitality, create a "down-home" atmosphere with the best of "up-town" service. Their seafood and other entrées are served in true Southern tradition. Delectable!

The restaurant traces its ancestry back to the 1930's and Boss Brice, a neighbor of Marjorie Rawlings. Boss had a place for hunters and fishermen to enjoy the fish and game they caught. Staying for a lazy weekend, in one of the Hermans' cozy cottages (with no sign of a telephone anywhere!), I couldn't help but share the anticipation of the gamesmen, as they watched their catch being cooked to perfection.

In much the same manner, Yearling patrons sample the hearty repast. The most popular entrée is the *Cross Creek Special* which consists of luscious catfish, succulent frog legs and fried "Cooter." For those not familiar with "Cooter," it is a soft shelled turtle, and a favorite of the locals. Also on the menu is a variety of fresh fish, breaded and fried until crispy and brown. Homestyle favorites include various individually prepared dishes, such as *Pan Fried Quail* and *Fried Alligator Tail* (under a new policy of the Florida Freshwater Fish and Game Commission).

Winner of several Florida Trend Golden Spoon Awards, the Yearling attracts people from as far away as the southern tip of Florida to enjoy the well known victuals and rural surroundings.

Marjorie Rawlings once said, "Cross Creek belongs to the wind and the rain, to the sun and the seasons, to the cosmic secrecy of seed, and beyond all, to time."

Relive these famous words echoed by one with a true love for this land of the "Florida Crackers" by dining at The Yearling.

On State Road 325, between 346 and 301, about 20 miles south of Gainesville.

No Reservations on Weekends.

HUSHPUPPIES
(Allow 30 minutes to 1 hour to rise)

2	onions (chopped)
1¼	cups self-rising corn meal
2½-3 oz. grapefruit juice	
1	T. baking powder
1½	cups self-rising flour
¼	cup + 1 T. sugar
	frying oil

1. Mix all ingredients except oil together. Mixture will be dry. Coat top with oil. Let rise 30 minutes-1 hour.
2. Shape into walnut size balls. Fry in oil, taking care that the inside cooks and the outside is golden brown.
3. Sprinkle with salt.

Yield: 3-4 dozen
Preparation: 1 hour/5 minutes
Cooking: 5-15 minutes

"Old fashioned goodness!"

— NOTES —

CROSS CREEK LIME PIE
(Allow time to chill in refrigerator)

2   cans Eagle-Brand sweetened-condensed milk
        zest*of 2 limes (grated rind)
1/3   cup lime juice (may use frozen)
3   egg yolks (beaten)
1½   t. 151 proof rum
        dash of orange bitters
4-6   drops green food coloring
1   9" graham cracker crust
½   pt. cream (whipped with 2 T. confectioner's sugar and
          1 T. rum)

1.   Add zest*and juice to condensed milk.Beat in egg yolks.
2.   Add rum, bitters and coloring. Pour into pie shell and
        top with whipped cream. Chill until set.

*See Glossary
Serves: 8
Preparation: 15 minutes
Chill: 4 hours

"The Yearling is famous for this delicious dessert!"

— NOTES —

GLOSSARY OF TERMS

GLOSSARY OF TERMS

Al dente
>To cook until barely tender, such as pasta.

Bearnaise Sauce (Blender)
>4 egg yolks
>½ t. salt
>1/8 t. cayenne pepper
>1 cup butter (melted)
>
>2 T. lemon juice
>2 t. minced onion
>2 t. minced parsley
>2 t. fresh tarragon or 1 t. dried

>1. With blender or food processor, beat yolks until thick. Add salt and cayenne.
>2. Add melted butter a little at a time, beating constantly.
>3. Add remaining ingredients and beat well. Serve while warm.
>   Yield: 1½ cups
>   Prep. time: 5 minutes

Bearnaise Sauce (Classic)
>To ¾ cup hollandaise (recipe in this section) add 1 T. tarragon vinegar and 1 t. each: chopped fresh parsley, tarragon and chervil. Serve with broiled meats and fish.

Blanch
>To parboil and then shock in cold water.

Bechamel (see Cream Sauce)

Bordelaise Sauce
>A sauce made from brown sauce or Sauce Espanole by adding red wine.
>2 T. shallots (minced)
>2 T. butter
>¾ cup red wine
>1½ cups brown sauce or
>   canned brown gravy
>   (Heinz)
>
>2 T. lemon juice
>2 T. parsley (minced)
>salt and pepper to taste
>mushroom (sliced) optional

>1. Sauté shallots in butter until transparent.
>2. Add wine and simmer until reduced by ½.
>3. Add remaining ingredients and heat.

Brown Sauce/Sauce Espanole
>A rich beef stock reduced and thickened with roux. May be purchased as beef gravy.

Beurre Manie'
>1 t. flour mixed with 1 t. butter—for thickening soups and sauces. Make a dozen of these little balls and freeze to be used as needed.

Butterfly

To cut against the grain or to cut lengthwise, leaving meat attached on one side. This is done for appearance and to tenderize.

Caramelize

To melt sugar until it is liquid and light brown.

Chop/Dice/Mince

Chop = ¼" cubes
Dice = 1/8" cubes
Mince = smallest cubes.

Clarify/Clarified

To make butter clear by heating and removing all whey or sediment as it rises to the top. Then carefully strain.

Court Bouillon

Highly seasoned fish broth (see fish stock).

Cream Sauce/or Béchamel

White sauce made with milk.

1 T. butter	1 cup hot milk
1 T. flour	salt, pepper, nutmeg to taste

1. Make roux of butter and flour. Cook until frothy, about 2 minutes.
2. Remove from heat. Slowly whisk in hot milk until smooth.
3. Cook 1 minute more and season.
    Yield: 1 cup.

Cream Sauce is Béchamel made with cream instead of milk.
Velouté is Béchamel made with white stock (such as chicken, veal or fish) in place of milk.

Créme Fraîche

To make this slightly soured cream, you add 1 tablespoon buttermilk to 1 cup heavy cream. Let sit in warm place overnight—or about 8-12 hours until thick.

Crêpes

Thin pancakes.
(for blender or food processor)

3-4 eggs	1 cup flour
1½ cups milk	½ t. salt
3 T. butter (melted)	

1. Combine all ingredients in processor and blend until smooth. Allow batter to rest 1 hour before frying. May be kept in refrigerator for 1 week.
2. 2 T. for each crepe in a 6 inch pan.

De-glaze
To pour liquid (such as wine, water or stock) in a cooking pan, scraping sides and bottom to loosen residue used in sauce.

Demi-Glace
Half-glaze/A reduced brown sauce.

Dredge/Dust/Flour
To dip in or sprinkle lightly with flour.

Fillet/Filet
Boneless meat or fish. To remove bones from fish.

Fish Stock/Court Bouillon
Trimmings and scraps from fish
1-2 onions
parsley stems, 1 carrot, 1 stalk celery
1 cup white wine
2 cups water

1. Simmer 20 minutes and strain.

Flambé/Flame
To cover food lightly with spirits and carefully ignite. It is to add flavor or spectacular beauty when serving.

Hollandaise Sauce (Blender)
3 egg yolks   dash of cayenne
2 t. lemon juice   ½ cup butter (melted)
¼ t. salt

1. In blender or food processor, beat yolks until thickened. Beat in juice, salt and cayenne.
2. Pour in hot butter, in a stream with machine running. Serve in warmed bowl.
    Yield: 1 cup

Hollandaise Sauce (Classic)
¾ cup butter   4 t. lemon juice
3   egg yolks (beaten)   dash of salt & cayenne

1. In top of double boiler, melt 1/3 butter. Beat in eggs and juice with wire whisk.
2. Add remaining butter slowly, beating constantly until mixture thickens—never allowing water to boil.
3. Stir in seasonings and serve.
    Yield: ¾ cup

Julienne
To cut into thin matchstick-like strips.

Mousseline Sauce

Add ½ cup whipped cream to 1 cup hollandaise just before serving.

Poach

To simmer gently in hot liquid, to cover.

Purée

To force food through a sieve or blend in food processor until smooth.

Reduce

To cook or simmer a liquid until it is less; to concentrate flavor.

Roux

An equal amount of butter and flour cooked a few minutes until smooth. Used to thicken.

Sauté

To cook in shallow pan, in small amount of butter or fat.

Score

To make shallow cuts in surface of meat.

Veal Stock

veal bones & scraps	thyme
1 carrot	white pepper
1 onion	salt
1 parsley sprig	2 cups water

1. Simmer for about 3-4 hours. Strain.

Zest

Grated rind of citrus.

Chowders (See Soups)

Crepes

D

Desserts

Duckling

E

Escargot

If you enjoyed *FAMOUS FLORIDA!*™
RESTAURANTS & RECIPES™ **you'll love:**

The cookbook and guide features a collection of Florida's "backwoods" dining, down-home cooking, big portions, and low prices. The restuarants selected are more than just eating establishments — they are statements of Florida's heritage. The restaurant owners have contributed stories about Florida'a past, its tradition in food preparations and customs. Recipes include how to prepare Florida's abundant native fruits and vegetables. You'll also enjoy the preparation suggestions for rattlesnake, soft-shell turtle, clam chowder, and more. And, of course, you'll find Florida's best recipe for Key lime pie, straight from the Keys!

ORDER FORM

Send to: LaFRAY PUBLISHING COMPANY,
　　　　　P.O. Box 7326, St. Petersburg, Florida 33734
　　　　　Phone: (813) 821-3233

Please send me:

＿＿＿＿ copies of **FAMOUS FLORIDA!**™
　　　　Restaurants & Recipes @ $9.95 each　　　$ ＿＿＿＿＿＿
＿＿＿＿ copies of **FAMOUS FLORIDA!**™
　　　　Underground Gourmet @ $9.95 each　　　$ ＿＿＿＿＿＿
　　　　Add postage and handling @ $1.50 each　　$ ＿＿＿＿＿＿
　　　　Florida residents add 5% sales tax @ $.55 each　$ ＿＿＿＿＿＿
　　　　　　　　　　　　　TOTAL ENCLOSED　$ ＿＿＿＿＿＿

Send to: LaFRAY PUBLISHING COMPANY,
　　　　　P.O. Box 7326, St. Petersburg, Florida 33734
　　　　　Phone: (813) 821-3233

Please send me:

＿＿＿＿ copies of **FAMOUS FLORIDA!**™
　　　　Restaurants & Recipes @ $9.95 each　　　$ ＿＿＿＿＿＿
＿＿＿＿ copies of **FAMOUS FLORIDA!**™
　　　　Underground Gourmet @ $9.95 each　　　$ ＿＿＿＿＿＿
　　　　Add postage and handling @ $1.50 each　　$ ＿＿＿＿＿＿
　　　　Florida residents add 5% sales tax @ $.55 each　$ ＿＿＿＿＿＿
　　　　　　　　　　　　　TOTAL ENCLOSED　$ ＿＿＿＿＿＿

Send to: LaFRAY PUBLISHING COMPANY,
　　　　　P.O. Box 7326, St. Petersburg, Florida 33734
　　　　　Phone: (813) 821-3233

Please send me:

＿＿＿＿ copies of **FAMOUS FLORIDA!**™
　　　　Restaurants & Recipes @ $9.95 each　　　$ ＿＿＿＿＿＿
＿＿＿＿ copies of **FAMOUS FLORIDA!**™
　　　　Underground Gourmet @ $9.95 each　　　$ ＿＿＿＿＿＿
　　　　Add postage and handling @ $1.50 each　　$ ＿＿＿＿＿＿
　　　　Florida residents add 5% sales tax @ $.55 each　$ ＿＿＿＿＿＿
　　　　　　　　　　　　　TOTAL ENCLOSED　$ ＿＿＿＿＿＿